Joy Within His House

# JOY

## —— WITHIN ——

# His House

A Cloistered Nun's
Reflections on
Following Christ

**Sr. Mary Magdalene of the
Immaculate Conception Prewitt, OP**

Our Sunday Visitor
Huntington, Indiana

*Nihil Obstat*
Msgr. Michael Heintz, Ph.D.
*Censor Librorum*

*Imprimatur*
✠ Kevin C. Rhoades
Bishop of Fort Wayne-South Bend
May 21, 2025

The *Nihil Obstat* and *Imprimatur* are official declarations that a book is free from doctrinal or moral error. It is not implied that those who have granted the *Nihil Obstat* and *Imprimatur* agree with the contents, opinions, or statements expressed.

Scripture texts in this work are taken from the *Revised Standard Version of the Bible*—Second Catholic Edition (Ignatius Edition) Copyright © 2006 National Council of the Churches of Christ in the United States of America. Used by permission. All rights reserved worldwide.

Excerpts from the *New Revised Standard Version Bible*: Catholic Edition, copyright © 1989, 1993 National Council of the Churches of Christ in the United States of America. Used by permission. All rights reserved worldwide.

Excerpts from the *New American Bible*, revised edition © 2010, 1991, 1986, 1970 Confraternity of Christian Doctrine, Washington, D.C. and are used by permission of the copyright owner. All Rights Reserved. No part of the New American Bible may be reproduced in any form without permission in writing from the copyright owner.

Excerpts from the English translation of the *Catechism of the Catholic Church* for use in the United States of America Copyright © 1994, United States Catholic Conference, Inc.—Libreria Editrice Vaticana. Used with Permission. English translation of the *Catechism of the Catholic Church*: Modifications from the Editio Typica copyright © 1997, United States Conference of Catholic Bishops—Libreria Editrice Vaticana.

Every reasonable effort has been made to determine copyright holders of excerpted materials and to secure permissions as needed. If any copyrighted materials have been inadvertently used in this work without proper credit being given in one form or another, please notify Our Sunday Visitor in writing so that future printings of this work may be corrected accordingly.

Our Sunday Visitor Publishing Division
Our Sunday Visitor, Inc.
200 Noll Plaza
Huntington, IN 46750
www.osv.com
1-800-348-2440

ISBN: 978-1-63966-221-0 (Inventory No. T2909)
1. RELIGION—Monasticism.
2. RELIGION—Christian Living—Spiritual Growth.
3. RELIGION—Christianity—Catholic.

eISBN: 978-1-63966-222-7
LCCN: 2025944934

Cover and interior design: Amanda Falk
Cover and interior art: AdobeStock, Photographs by Jeffrey Bruno. Supplemental images from the Monastery of Our Lady of the Rosary, as noted

PRINTED IN THE UNITED STATES OF AMERICA

*Dedicated in Honor of*

*Our Lady of the Rosary, Saint Dominic,
and Saint Mary Magdalene*

*Under their patronage, may this book
bring all who read it closer to Christ.*

# Contents

Introduction ••• 8

1. Monastic Elements ••• 18

2. Common Life ••• 38

3. Liturgical Prayer ••• 60

4. Dominican Prayer ••• 74

5. Evangelical Counsels ••• 100

6. Hearing and Keeping the Word of God ••• 122

7. Study ••• 136

8. Work ••• 154

9. Withdrawal from the World ••• 168

10. Penitential Practices ••• 184

11. Government ••• 202

12. Recreation ••• 212

13. Our Lady ••• 224

Conclusion ••• 234

Acknowledgments ••• 239

Appendix I: Stages of Formation ••• 241

Appendix II: Glossary of Terms ••• 243

Photo Captions ••• 247

Notes ••• 251

# Introduction

"How does a girl from Kansas end up in a monastery in New Jersey?" People ask me this question all the time.

My simple answer is, "God."

I started seriously discerning my religious vocation at age eighteen, while studying Graphic and Imaging Technology at Pittsburg State University in Pittsburg, Kansas. Riding my bike between my residence and classes, I would daydream about where I saw myself in ten years and was surprised to envision myself sitting at a desk in an office, unhappy. I thought, "Is this *really* what I want to do with my life? Is this really what *God* wants me to do with my life? Will I be happy doing *this* as a career?"

That undramatic bike ride had staying power, and the questions nagged. To distract myself from them, I made a few significant moves — changing houses, changing jobs, changing friends. I changed majors, started new hobbies, and began working full-time as a prep cook at Applebee's. I loved the environment and experience of working in a restaurant (which would turn out to be excellent preparation for community life, as you'll soon see). In my junior year, I was elected vice president of the Newman Center, a Catholic student group on campus, and became heavily involved in its activities. This commitment helped me to develop a deeper prayer life, which brought a measure of peace. I started attending Mass and praying a daily Rosary and even leading the Liturgy of the Hours. Honestly, it was the blind leading the blind, but jumping in was the best way to learn, and it really fed me.

As I grew in these new prayer habits, the answers to my earlier questions slowly unraveled. It's hard — well, basically impossible — to hear God if you aren't listening. I used to wake up at 6 in the morning and walk around the silent, still campus, just talking to God, and learning to listen. I confessed that certain things were not going as I'd hoped; I told Him about my hardships and worked on building a relationship with Him, and I had a real sense of being listened to and heard.

God knew I wasn't ready for everything all at once, so He prepared me for the answers in small doses.

Through prayer, adoration, and daily Mass, thoughts of religious life began to arise. "What? *Me?* What a crazy idea! Utterly nuts!"

Initially, I was terrified. But I began to pray about it and realized that if this was indeed what God wanted for me, then I wanted it too.

Around this time, I began to pray the Rosary daily, entrusting my vocational queries to the patronage of Our Lady of the Rosary. I'd jumped into the breach and conceded that perhaps I was being called to serve as a religious, so the question became, "Doing what?"

Wading through *A Guide to Religious Ministries,* (informally known as the "Blue Book," which contains every religious community in the United States), I kept seeing the weirdly old-fashioned word, *cloistered*. I asked the Newman Center priest, "What does this word mean? I thought all the cloisters died out in the Middle Ages!" He arranged for me to visit some cloistered Carmelites a few hours away, and I discovered that cloisters (monasteries) still existed.

You too may be confused about what a cloister is, as the word can have several different meanings. In this context, it denotes that a nun (or monk) lives in a monastery dedicated totally to God. Cloistered religious stay within the premises of the monastic space, and their sole apostolate is to grow closer to God and to pray for others.

I asked the Carmelite nuns every question I could think of, learned much about their life, and enjoyed the visit. Driving home, I thought, "These women are *nuts!* ... and I think I might be nuts too." I loved their devotion to prayer, to Our Lady, to silence, penance, and simple work, and their thirst for the salvation of souls.

The visit convinced me that God *might* be calling me to the cloistered life, after all, and gave me a deepening appreciation of Our Lord's words, "You did not choose me but I chose you" (Jn 15:16).

Unthinkable as it seemed, I accepted the notion outright. I began to ask God what community would help me grow the most in happiness and holiness and looked at all the major religious orders — Carmelites, Franciscans, Benedictines, Dominicans — as well as smaller associations and communities, and became attracted to the charism and spirituality of the Dominicans, formally known as the Order of Preachers. I loved their emphasis on study, truth, and devotion to Our Lady. Their attention to, and fostering of, a preaching and missionary spirit within a cloistered enclosure intrigued me. It seemed like a perfect fit.

So, I began to write to Dominican cloistered communities in the United States. There were fourteen monasteries at that time, and I wrote to every one of them. I heard the words of the liturgy as if they were spoken directly to me: "Be patient a little while longer" (Rv 6:11, NAB).

Fifty-seven days into praying the Rosary daily, I found myself on the doorstep of the Monastery of Our Lady of the Rosary in Summit, New Jersey, thinking, "What could be better than a monastery dedicated to continuously praying and meditating on the life of Christ through the Rosary, in an order founded by Saint Dominic, the man with whom devotion to the Rosary began?" As has happened with many in my community, when I walked into the chapel and saw Jesus in the Blessed Sacrament, I had a strong sense in my gut that this was the place for me.

As part of my "live-in experience," I spent two weeks living with the community within the enclosure, getting a taste of monastic life and the rhythms of prayer, work, study, and community. I discovered that, yes, I desired this sort of life. I could see myself living it.

When the visit was over, I found that I missed it.

Of course, my discernment didn't end there, nor did the community's discernment of me. The process continued, step-by-step, daily asking God, "Is this what you want for me? Please give me the grace."

As one of our wise, older sisters used to say, "When God calls you, you go!" She was referring both to religious life and eternal life, but I heard Him calling me to the former and thus — when the community and I both decided it was time — to New Jersey I went!

• • •

When I first sat in our monastery's enormous public chapel, I'd been filled with an intense desire to get inside, to become part of the life behind the grille — the monastic threshold of separation and encounter. When I did, at last, join the monastery, fourteen of my family members and friends were present.

Entrance to a monastery involves a very simple ceremony: The woman who joins is led by the prioress into the area where the nuns live and pray, the

cloistered area also known as the enclosure. As I walked through the door and entered the nuns' choir (our side of the chapel, which adjoins the public sanctuary), the faces of my friends and family were pressed up against the grille, looking around and trying to see inside. As nuns, once we enter, our lives become hidden. For good reasons, this mysterious, concealed life sparks curiosity in layfolk, and I am often asked for insight into how the life we live as nuns can help one to grow in holiness in his own life.

Perhaps you are not even aware that thousands of women dedicated to praying for you are scattered throughout the world, hidden in many different cloisters. The lives of these women are "mysteriously fruitful for the growth of the people of God."[1] Because our daily lives build up a closeness to the Lord, monastic nuns stand as mediators in Christ, the One Mediator, between heaven and earth (1 Tm 2:5). Our lives of withdrawal and prayer permit us to intercede with God each day on behalf of the whole world, and in this unique way, we support our brothers and sisters who actively preach the Gospel and all who need prayers.

Like the early Christian community (Acts 4:32), we keep all things in common so that, united in heart and soul, we can serve God constantly by listening to His Word and worshiping Him in the "breaking of the bread" (Acts 2:42) and in communal prayer. We are greatly aided by the evangelical counsels as we make our vows of poverty, chastity, and obedience. We are dedicated to living an enclosed monastic life, which includes the common life, the celebration of the liturgy and private prayer, the observance of the vows, and the study of sacred truth. To fulfill these faithfully, we are helped by enclosure, silence, the religious habit, work, and penitential practices (LCM 35, II). Central to our cloistered life is our common goal of union with God, which is what brings us to the monastery in the first place.

The principles of monastic life can be an inspiration and example for lay people seeking to draw nearer to the Lord. Pope Francis, in his apostolic constitution *Vultum Dei quaerere,* addresses contemplative sisters, saying, "The world needs you every bit as much as a sailor on the high seas needs a beacon to guide him to a safe haven."[2]

In other words, contemplative nuns are essential and necessary for the world today because we can point toward God. Using my own experience and the wisdom of countless other women who have gone before me, in the

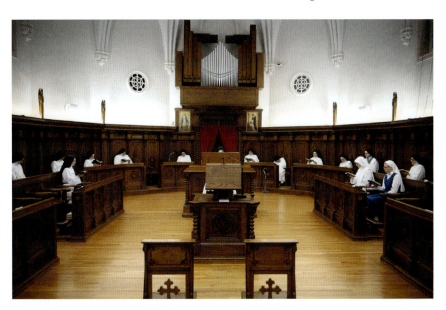

subsequent chapters we will cover all the elements essential to the monastic life of Dominican nuns and suggest how they can aid you in your pursuit of heaven. As we examine these elements, remember that they are not isolated components; rather, one leads into the other and back again. Like threads in a tapestry, they work together as an organic whole.

Thank you for picking up this book, which was emphatically not written by a saint. As you read, please remember that we nuns still have all the same problems as "regular people," like you. We may have all the necessary helps to become saints, for "my grace is sufficient for you" (2 Cor 12:9), but still, we are sinners. We fall and we get back up, and that is the central message of the Christian life, as the *Catechism* tells us: "The Gospel is the revelation in Jesus Christ of God's mercy to sinners."[3]

This text offers those who live on the other side of the cloister wall the simple experience of those who live within. I hope that you will be able to draw from our principles and practices some help in your own daily life. More than anything, I want to share with you the joy that I find in living the life of a Dominican nun, of which our Constitutions relate:

> The nuns seek God by observing the norms of the purely contemplative life, by maintaining their withdrawal from the world by enclosure and silence, by working diligently, studying the truth eagerly, searching the Scriptures with ardent heart, praying intently, willingly practicing penance, pursuing communion through their manner of government, in purity of conscience and the joy of sisterly concord, "in freedom of spirit." (LCM 1, V)

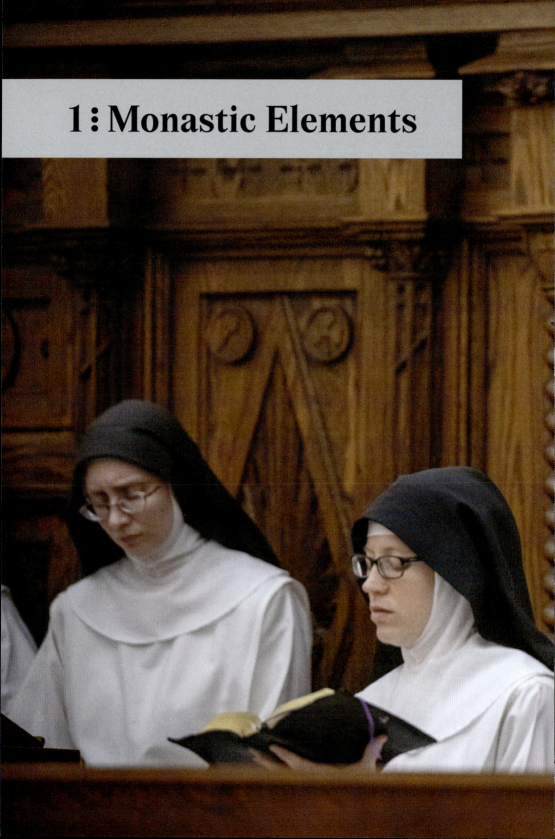

# 1: Monastic Elements

•••

*I came that they may have life,*
*and have it abundantly.*

*— John 10:10*

•••

Before forming the Order of Preachers, Saint Dominic was a Canon Regular — a cathedral priest who followed the Rule of Saint Augustine, lived a common life, and was dedicated to private and liturgical prayer. Dominican spirituality is rooted in monasticism, thanks to Saint Dominic's experiences as a canon.

A monastery is a building or collection of buildings occupied by a community of monks or nuns living under religious vows. Monasticism is the religious way of life, involving renouncing worldly pursuits for the sake of spiritual goods. It has evolved from the fourth century, when early monastics headed out to the desert to find a secluded, quiet way to live the Gospel and to follow Christ more radically. The story of one of the earliest known desert monks, St. Anthony of Egypt, tells that he walked into a church and, upon hearing the proclaimed words of Jesus, "If you would be perfect, go, sell what you possess and give to the poor, and you will have treasures in heaven; and come, follow me" (Mt 19:21), took the command literally. He immediately sold everything he had so he could go to the desert and live for God alone. The words of Scripture speak of this experience: "I will allure her, / and bring her into the wilderness, / and speak tenderly to her" (Hos 2:14).

We cloistered religious also go to the "desert" to seek God. Just as Jesus "was led up by the Spirit into the wilderness" (Mt 4:1), we too are led to the desert wilderness of the monastery to encounter God. We do not run *from* the world, but *to* someone, and that someone is Jesus Christ.

A fruitful monastic vocation means to be fast-knit to Christ, united in charity (see LCM 74, IV). Becoming one with Christ takes time and growth in self-knowledge, which can be challenging — one who enters the monastery experiences a new and deep call to humility, obedience, and disciplined charity. The more complete the gift of self, the greater the fruitfulness.

In a broader sense, every vocation demands surrender and is fruitful to the extent that we embrace that surrender. To follow Christ is to imitate His example of self-emptying, to take up our own crosses and follow Him.

The monastic life requires a certain self-emptying in imitation of Christ, who "though he was in the form of God, did not count equality with God a thing to be grasped, but emptied himself, taking the form of a servant, being born in the likeness of men. And being found in human form, he humbled himself and became obedient unto death, even death on a cross" (Phil 2:6–8). Our lives pass through the cross to the Resurrection because we know that where we are going, Christ has gone before.

Self-giving is an intense act of love, which must drive all we do. The surrender of self brings about an effusive joy that cannot be contained as we pursue God, who is All Good.

Understandably, it can be difficult to see the meaning or purpose of this life. In Willa Cather's novel *Shadows on the Rock*, the character Auclair reflects on how a priest's vow of dedication to the missionary territory of seventeenth-century Quebec seems a waste of his gifts and talents. Then he adds, "Perhaps that is the box of precious ointment which was acceptable to the Savior, and I am like the disciple who thought it might have been used better in another way."[1] Any of us can easily fall into this Judas mentality of trying to judge the worth of how we, or others, should spend their lives, but ultimately we will not know the value of our vocations until the judgment. Christ is the only judge, and in this story, "her sins, which are many, are forgiven, for she loved much" (Lk 7:47).

Seeking God is always worth the sacrifice, even when we cannot see the effects, which is particularly relevant to the cloistered life. Jesus said, "Everyone who has left houses or brothers or sisters or father or mother or children or fields, for my name's sake, will receive a hundredfold, and will inherit eternal life" (Mt 19:29). Before we can receive the hundredfold, we must first endure the sorrow, discomfort, and difficulty of separation — from family, friends, possessions, goods, future goods, and property. It's a hardship, but one that permits a new freedom from obligations, social commitments, and ties.

To begin, we will discuss the Augustinian roots and Dominican aspects that are foundational to our life, as well as the cell, the habit, community exhortations to live the Gospel, and the refectory. Later, we will cover enclosure, penitential practices, and silence, which also make up regular observance.

"Regular observance," or the observance of the Augustinian Rule, en-

capsulates all the elements of our life. It is the concrete, necessary observances or customary practices that breathe the Holy Spirit into our actions and help us to "to follow Christ more closely and ... to live more effectively [our] contemplative life in the Order of Preachers" (LCM 35, I).

## Augustinian Roots

Each religious community has a Rule it follows — a guide and help in structuring our daily life and living in a particular way. More than a set of restrictive rules, it is an aid for spiritual growth and progress. Dominicans have followed the Rule of Saint Augustine since our foundation in the thirteenth century. This brief Rule, written by the well-known bishop of Hippo who had himself lived in a monastic community, features eight short chapters that are timeless enough to be as applicable to modern monastics as it was to the men and women of the fifth century. They cover:

1. Common life
2. Prayer
3. Moderation and self-denial
4. Chastity and fraternal correction
5. The care of community goods and treatment of the sick
6. Asking pardon and forgiving offenses
7. Governance and obedience
8. Observance of the rule

Augustine's Rule reflects the life of the apostles as they imitated Christ and sought to live out the Gospel — a harmonious common life which Augustine summarized in this way: "The main purpose for your having come together is to live harmoniously in your house, intent upon God in oneness of mind and heart."[2] The simple principles found in the Rule of Saint Augustine form the foundation for Dominicans living in charity, love of God and neighbor, in that very "oneness of mind and heart."

## Dominican Aspects

While every baptized Christian is called to live *a* contemplative life — a life of prayer — cloistered nuns live *the* contemplative life in the strictest sense — a life entirely ordered around prayer. The unique mission of the whole Dominican order, however, is associated with "holy preaching" for the salvation of souls, and we contemplatives serve that mission not through an external apostolate, but through our life of prayer and penance.

Saint Dominic was born about 1172 in Caleruega, Spain, to Felix de Guzman and Jane of Aza, who was beatified in 1828. At an early age, Dominic was sent to train for the priesthood under an uncle. Upon completing his schooling, he joined the Cathedral Chapter of Canons Regular at Osma in Spain. In 1206, he went with Bishop Diego on a diplomatic trip and began his life's mission after encountering the Albigensian heresy through his travels. This heresy, and its allied branch known as Catharism, held that there were two gods: one who created the spiritual world and was good and another who created the material world and was evil. This dualistic view led the Cathars to the conclusion that procreation was evil because it prolonged materiality and that suicide was good because it ended it. The goal of Catharism was to liberate the soul from the body. Dominic was so moved by the plight of those steeped in this error that he dedicated his entire life to preaching against this error and bringing others back to the true faith.

Shortly after Dominic began his preaching missions, nine young women who were converted from Catharism gathered to live the religious life under his direction. Saint Dominic established his first monastery of nuns in 1206 at the Monastery of Prouilhe, in the Diocese of Toulouse, France. Legend holds that on the evening of July 22, 1206, the feast of St. Mary Magdalene, Dominic saw a fireball pass through the sky as he sat near the villages of Prouilhe and Fanjeaux. The flaming ball was like a comet that hovered over the Church of Notre Dame de Prouilhe before disappearing. Dominic saw this same sign on two consecutive nights and took it as a blessing from the Virgin Mary, to establish the monastery there. This sign became known as the *Seignadou*, meaning "sign of God."

Only after establishing these female converts did Dominic begin to attract men to himself to preach and teach for the salvation of souls. As the community grew, they unanimously chose to live by the Rule of Saint

Augustine and sought approval from the Holy Father. On December 22, 1216, Pope Honorius III formally approved the new Order of Preachers.

Before this time, monks and nuns stayed solely in their monastic communities and did not engage in active apostolates, which were reserved for parish priests.[3] But the Holy Spirit was moving in the Church, inspiring Dominic and St. Francis of Assisi to found the mendicant, or begging, orders. Both saints embraced a life of evangelical poverty as a witness to the faith, attracting converts in a way previous preachers had not. While the Franciscans embraced manual labor and outreach, Dominic's friars would be preachers of the Word who remained devoted to study. This kept them connected to their monastic roots, dedicated to the prayer and contemplation that supported their preaching.

After the first house of nuns in Prouilhe was established, Dominic founded two more monasteries for women, in Rome and Madrid. In fact, the only description of Saint Dominic's physical appearance that we have comes to us from one of the nuns at the monastery in Rome. This nun, Blessed Cecilia Cesarini, tells us,

> He was of medium height: his figure supple, his face handsome and slightly sanguine, his hair and beard blond with a slight reddish tinge, his eyes beautiful. From his brow and eyes there emanated a certain radiant splendor which won the admiration and veneration of all. He always appeared joyous and smiling except when moved with compassion at some affliction of his neighbor. His hands were long and handsome and his powerful voice noble and sonorous. He was not in the least bald and wore the religious tonsure entire, sprinkled with a few white hairs.[4]

Only a woman would give such a lengthy description, while conveying his joyful, compassionate nature, and we are grateful she did!

Saint Dominic's successor as Master of the Order, Blessed Jordan, is attributed to have said of Dominic, "He showed himself everywhere to be a man of the gospel in word and deed. No one was more accessible to his brethren and companions, no one was more pleasant, the best and greatest counselor."

Dominic died on August 6, 1221. Over the last 800-plus years, Dominican monastic life has continued to grow and thrive, and Saint Dominic continues to watch over us. Today, cloistered Dominican nuns throughout the world still live the form of life established by Saint Dominic at Prouilhe, Rome, and Madrid. Worldwide, there are currently over 2,000 professed cloistered nuns, with around fifty postulants and fifty novices in approximately 180 monasteries.[5]

## The Cell

The words *monk* and *monastery* come from the Greek *monos* meaning "single" or "one" (meaning those who dwell alone, though within a community). I often forget how strange it sounds when I casually mention that I live in a cell — people automatically assume the negative connotation of a prison cell. However, the word simply comes from the Latin word *cella,* meaning "room." The monastic cell is a private place for rest, prayer, and study, containing a bed, a desk with a chair, and a bookshelf.

The cell is a place where we can be alone with Christ in solitude, as per our Constitutions (the book of guidance and law particular to our order, to be lived according to our charism under the umbrella of the Church): "The monastic cell is not only a place for rest, but like an enclosure within the enclosure it is a closed room for prayer in secret, a place for *lectio divina*, meditation, study or individual work" (LCM 50).

There is a story of the Desert Fathers in which a brother came to Abba Moses and asked him for advice. Abba Moses said to him, "Go, sit in your cell, and your cell will teach you everything." The wisdom of this statement has always struck me, because it is very difficult to sit in your cell by yourself for long periods of time. Yet it is often what we need and how we learn, because it allows us to avoid some distractions and become vulnerable before God. Sitting in silence in my cell has often led to prayers of praise for God's goodness, recalling His many blessings. Other times, it has led to introspection and recognition of my own shortcomings — recalling words I should not have said, times I could have been kinder in my responses, or things I should have said and did not.

Sometimes, there is a restlessness that can occur in the cell — I cannot

focus on what I am trying to read, and I must pause and ask myself, "What's really the issue here?" Then, the interior conversation begins. Confronting this restlessness, whether enclosed or not, allows us to listen to an inner turmoil that has gone unheard in the constant noise of our distractions.

The cell is a sacred space of solitude, silence, and prayer; one can pray in silent solitude, really in *any* room, but a cell is different. It is our own, but in the truest sense, it is shared with Him. The simplicity of the cell facilitates the important virtue of orderliness, among other virtues. I have found the adage "a clean room is a clean mind" to be true. The clean cell is something I am always working toward, realizing that I sleep better at night if my desk is clear. It means that I am living in the day and can "let the day's own trouble be sufficient" (Mt 6:34).

Augustine famously defined peace as "the tranquility of order" (see CCC 2304). When we are peaceful in our cells, the peace flows into our lives. The same is true when our desires are rightly oriented to God, because God has ordered all things well. When there is chaos in our lives, it is hard to sit quietly in our cells, but that is when we most need to be alone with God.

## The Habit

As consecrated Dominican religious, we wear a traditional all-white habit, as briefly defined in the Constitutions: "The habit of the nuns, which is a sign of their consecration and a witness to poverty, consists of a white tunic, a belt with a rosary attached, a white scapular and a black veil and cappa" (LCM 59). We wear the habit as a sign of our consecration to God, a visible reminder to us and to the people of God that we are set apart for His service, a sign of hope that one can live joyfully dedicated to God through poverty, chastity, and obedience. The habit is a witness to poverty in its imitation of Christ — its simplicity, modesty, and commonality do not attract attention or prestige, but proclaim who we are and what we believe.

The second section of the Constitutions instructs us to wear the habit at all times, along with the black cappa (a kind of cloak) for solemn occasions. The habit is white as a reminder of our baptism and consecration, reminiscent of the white garment worn by infants or catechumens, and of our desire for purity. The black signifies mortification, penance, or death to the world. The white tunic is a long garment, similar to a graduation gown, with really long sleeves that are folded up. The white scapular is a long, rectangular piece of cloth with a hole that fits over the head; it hangs over the shoulders and covers the front and back of the tunic. A Sister first receives the habit at her Vestition (clothing) ceremony when she officially begins her novitiate. As a novice, her veil is white.

The black veil received at profession is a witness to our commitment to Christ and a sign of our consecration; when we put it on each morning, we pray, "He has placed a seal upon my brow that I may admit no other lover but Him." The veil attaches to the white guimpe, which is like a head sock with a hole for the face that goes over the head and covers the neck and shoulders.

Our habits remind us of God and why we have come to the monastery. The Primitive Constitutions state, "Your clothing must not attract attention, since it is not for your clothing but for virtue and purity of soul that you ought to please. The glory of the king's daughter is from within."[6] This is an echo of Psalm 45:11, "The king will desire your beauty," and places the emphasis on poverty of spirit in clothing which, through virtue,

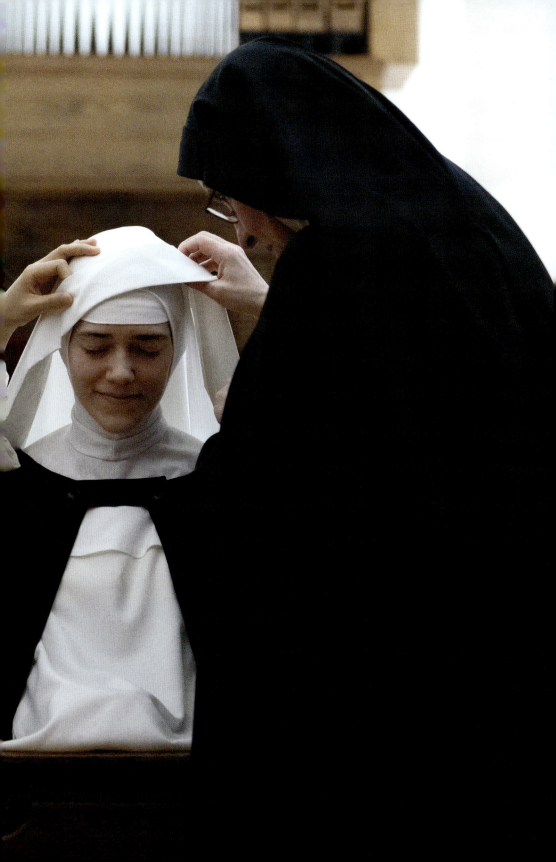

should foster interior virtue and spiritual beauty.

Obviously, the habit attracts more curiosity today than it did 800 years ago, but, contrasting the flamboyant styles of secular clothing, the religious habit should attract attention to God, not to us. The wearing of a habit communicates a religious' public commitment to follow Christ more closely, in a way dedicated and set aside for God.[7] The habit is a beautiful sign, a visual witness to others and a reminder to us. It draws attention to something beyond the physical — the sight of it makes people think about God. Personally, I feel so comfortable wearing the habit; I can't imagine wearing anything else now, and I love how it stands as a constant reminder that I belong to Christ. More than one sister has been asked by a little kid, "Are you a princess?" To which the natural reply is, "Yes, I am a Bride of Christ." The habit is a daily call to live up to what it means to belong to Christ and, at the same time, a testimony for others to the love of God.

There is also a story about the Blessed Virgin that makes the Dominican habit special. Near the beginning of the order, a Dominican friar named Bl. Reginald of Orleans had been suffering terrible fevers when one night the Queen of Heaven and Mother of Mercy appeared to him. She anointed his eyes, nose, ears, mouth, chest, navel, and feet with a soothing ointment and said, "I anoint your feet with a holy oil in preparation for the gospel of peace." Then, the Virgin Mary gave him the scapular of the order. Immediately, he became well. His cure was so miraculous that the physician who had been looking after him was baffled about his instantaneous recovery. Dominicans have held our white scapular as a revered gift from Our Lady ever since.[8]

## Regular Chapter

Most monasteries have in parallel structure a choir (the place we pray), a refectory (the place we eat), and a chapter hall (the place we gather as a community for examination and encouragement). In our chapter hall, at the front on the wall, there is a huge crucifix with a hand-carved wooden statue on each side: Mary on one side, Dominic on the other, exactly like in the choir. However, the Chapter Hall statue of Dominic is unique because Dominic is holding a set of wooden spoons. Why wooden spoons?

In 1219, Saint Dominic brought wooden spoons from Spain to the nuns at the monastery at Santa Maria in Tempulo, Rome. It is the custom in our monastery that each sister receives a wooden spoon when she enters as a reminder of the thoughtfulness and generosity of our holy father, Dominic.

There are many times when each of us fails to be kind, compassionate, or considerate to those around us, and there is a need to make restitution for these actions. From this same need for restitution and compassionate response, we gather in "regular chapter." Regular chapter is distinct from the *conventual chapter* which will be discussed in the section on government (and, to further the confusion, is usually just called "chapter").

Regular chapter is a non-authoritative gathering — a chance for us to come together once a month and examine how we are living out the Gospel. Our Constitutions say, "At the regular chapter the nuns gather as sisters in charity and humility under the leadership of the prioress to give one another mutual assistance in the renewal and development of the regular life" (LCM 68).

So what does this mutual assistance look like? The details of the regular chapter can vary from monastery to monastery. In our house, after offering a prayer for our benefactors, the prioress or a sister she selects gives a talk, which examines a particular aspect of our life. I have found much wisdom, encouragement, and insight from these talks. For example, a recent one on gratitude and the ways that criticism can negatively impact our awareness of God's providence inspired me to hold my tongue the next time I found myself about to complain about the weather. Instead, I was grateful for what God provided.

Since these talks are situated in a specific time and place, hearing the words of Scripture, the Constitutions, and the Rule of Saint Augustine together take on new meaning when presented from a different perspective or personality. The talk can help us examine unity, or how we are living the rule, or it can even prompt an examination of conscience.

Regular chapter continues with the "chapter of faults" at which sisters are free to publicly admit some minor infraction which impacts the common life. For instance, a sister can admit to speaking or being thoughtlessly noisy during times of silence. After the sisters who wish to share their

faults have spoken, all the sisters make the *venia* together. The *venia* is a prostration Dominicans make, where one lies on one's right side with the right hand under the head and the left hand flat on the ground by the stomach. It is a sign of profound humility as well as an act of penance. The regular chapter concludes by offering prayers together as a common penance for our faults.

Once, when I was in the novitiate, a sister was going through a tardiness phase; she was late for everything. Annoyed and distracted by it, I was becoming irritated with her. At our next chapter meeting, she stood up and accused herself of being late all the time because she was going through some difficulties. Instantly, my heart melted with compassion, and I was far more understanding about her lack of punctuality. The chapter of faults helps the whole community to grow in mercy for one another.

The chapter of faults within regular chapter is *not* an exercise in degrading ourselves or demoralizing our human dignity. Rather, as an undertaking of charity, it is a humble admission to something that most of the community has already observed with their eyes and ears. There is incredible freedom in standing up and saying, "I know I was late for Office and I'm sorry." Acknowledging our actions with verbal recognition gives us a greater sense of responsibility for what we did, and simultaneously we have the encouragement of being forgiven by the community because we are all working on becoming holier together.

Of course, the same principles apply to family life as well. One can immediately apologize to the group for burning the dinner or leaving a mess in the family room or not truly listening to someone. In a monastery or a family dwelling, an acknowledgment of a fault against the common good cuts the tension and allows us to move on and live together in peace.

I believe that the chapter of faults has at its root that command of the Lord to "show kindness and mercy to one another" (Zec 7:9), and as we read in the letter of Saint James, to "confess your sins to one another, and pray for one another, so that you may be healed" (5:16). Obviously, the Sacrament of Reconciliation is essential for confessing what is strictly sinful. However, there are actions we do, or neglect to do, that injure the common life. Admitting one's faults may sting sometimes, but the result is a flood of support and renewed respect for one another.

## Refectory

In the Church of Saint Sixtus in Rome, one day the friars had gone out begging but returned home empty-handed. They asked Saint Dominic what to do, as there were over a hundred friars to feed, and he commanded the brethren to sit down so they could pray. As soon as his prayer was finished, there appeared two beautiful young men in white with baskets of bread who distributed to each friar, beginning with the youngest, a loaf of bread. In their need, God provided — and this is why, in Dominican houses, the youngest eat first.

In the Eucharistic Banquet our souls are nourished, and in the refectory our bodies, as well as our souls, are nourished. We eat in silence as we listen to the Word of God or some spiritual reading or lecture, for "Man shall not live by bread alone, but by every word that proceeds from the mouth of God" (Mt 4:4). As Saint Paul says in the First Letter to the Corinthians, "So, whether you eat or drink, or whatever you do, do all to the glory of God" (1 Cor 10:31).

So even the act of eating is a training of our minds and hearts to give glory to God. We have the same wisdom from Saint Augustine, "Let not your mouths alone take nourishment but let your hearts too hunger for the word of God" (RA ch. 3, par. 15). Just as our stomach rumbles for bodily food, our souls are rumbling for spiritual nourishment. Through listening to substantial material while we eat, we have "food" for our hearts to "chew" on. Our refectory ceremonies, although simple, place our meals within a liturgical context. The prayers at grace change with the liturgical seasons and the rank of the day's feast.

What do nuns eat? Our meals are simple, but adequate for our needs. There are two cooked meals a day, a tradition which dates to the San Sisto Constitutions.[9] Breakfast for our community is usually bread or cereal. The one exception is Easter Monday, when we get a hot egg breakfast. (Other communities have different practices, even within the Dominican nuns.) Our midday meal is called dinner, not lunch, as it is our main meal. By contrast, we call our evening meal "supper," and it is smaller and lighter. We fast during Advent, Lent, and all Fridays of the year. For our community, Wednesdays, Fridays, all of Advent (except Sundays), and all of Lent are meatless.

Our diet is both regimented and diverse. We eat a variety of proteins, starches, and vegetables for noon, and a simple protein with a supplement (soup in the colder months) for supper, with items like salad, fruit, and yogurt always available. We will have special treats like cookies for saints and feasts — you appreciate ice cream (or spaghetti and meatballs) much more when you no longer have control over when you can eat them! In religious life I've eaten things I would have never dreamed of trying, like goat or tripe. One sister joined thinking she would never have pizza again. What do you think we had for supper the day she entered? Leftover pizza!

Eating together is a sign of our common life. It is important that this time be a sharing of bodily and spiritual nourishment. A wonderful line was carved into the table in Saint Augustine's community's refectory: "Whoever thinks that he is able to nibble at the life of absent friends, must know that he's unworthy of this table." Augustine is exhorting us not to speak ill of others when they are not present, "nibbling away at them," so to speak. An image of this comes from Dante's *Inferno*, Cantos 32–33, where we see the trapped-in-ice Count Ugolino eating the head of his en-

emy, the archbishop. In a similar way, we do not want to "chew" on those who are not physically present among us; rather we want to show charity for all, always. Since we would not intentionally disrespect the person of Christ, so too we do not want to intentionally disrespect our absent neighbor.

This quotation from Augustine also reflects the importance of being united as a community, always speaking charitably, and not mentioning in another's absence what we would not say in her presence. Thus, the unity we share in the common meal extends to charity throughout the day.

In our professions we promise obedience "according to the Rule of blessed Augustine and the Constitutions of the Nuns of the Order of Preachers." Through the common discipline of following this structure, routine, and practices, we seek union with God. These elements are adapted to time and place but have been proven to foster union with Christ and lead to salvation, for us and others. As the Fundamental Constitutions of the Order states, "All these practices contribute not only to the glory of God and our sanctification, but serve directly the salvation of mankind."[10]

# 2 : Common Life

•••

*Behold, how good and pleasant it is*
*when brothers dwell in unity!*

*— Psalm 133:1*

•••

Technically, all elements of monastic life constitute "common" life, but here let us focus on community and the dynamics that play out in living together.

Community is an excellent aid in growing and helping others toward Christ; for it is good and pleasant when brothers dwell in unity (see Ps 133:1). Since no one living is yet a saint, this life is often marked with the trials that come with loving others; there are growth spurts and flat times. Working toward a common goal, which is holiness, assists us in being encouraging and helpful toward one another as we strive to be "one mind and heart in God." In examining our own woundedness, we become aware of how much we stand in need of God's mercy, and that awareness leads us to a greater sense of gratitude and compassion for others. Charity forms the foundation for our monastic life, as we continually ask for mercy from God and one another.

The *Catechism* teaches, "Of all visible creatures, only man is 'able to know and love his creator'" (356). Because of our rational nature, we *choose* to love; it is an act of the will. Our coming to the cloister is a response to God, who first loved us, but our perseverance there is a daily repeated choice, made possible by His grace. We live out the love that is in our heart by our actions toward one another.

Living as consecrated women, monastics hold all things in common and share each other's joys and pains. Early in religious life, I experienced my first monastic funeral. I had spent the past year getting to know this dear, energetic, elderly sister and then one morning she had a stroke, passing peacefully in her sleep two months later. The death and burial of a religious is a bittersweet thing. On the one hand — glory to God — she's made it! She faithfully ran the race and crossed the finish line. She accomplished the shared purpose of our lives: to die and, God willing, be with Christ.

On the other hand, there is for the community a very real and natural aspect of sorrow, pain, and loss. Death confronts us with stark questions: How do we want to live, die, and be remembered? What is the goal we are striving for? The Psalmist gives the answer that I want: "But for me it is good to be near God" (Ps 73:28).

One evening, while praying the Rosary before the Blessed Sacrament, I glanced back at the beautiful wood carvings that adorn our choir. I was struck by the small metal plaque on the wall behind me, which reads, "Remember thy last end, and thou shalt never sin" (Sir 7:40, Douay-Rheims). This idea, known in the tradition of our faith as *memento mori,* is echoed in the Rule of St. Benedict, "Remember to keep death daily before your eyes."[1]

How does *memento mori* speak to the common life? As Christians, our goal is to know and love God perfectly in heaven — in one word, *beatitude,* or supreme blessedness. To reach that goal, religious take vows, whereby we commit ourselves to the life of perfection and organize ourselves into a stable community. This phrase "the life of perfection" pertains to bishops and religious, not that we are perfect, but that we are in a permanent state wherein we are aspiring to perfection.

Again, the monastic community is ultimately about its members becoming one heart and mind in God. This harmony flows into all the elements of our life and thus is an essential foundation on which to build; community life fosters and supports the contemplative life. As our Constitutions state, "This unity transcends the limits of the monastery and attains its fullness in communion with the order and with the whole Church of Christ" (LCM 2, I). At the heart of our Dominican monastic life is the following of Christ, *Sequela Christi.* By imitating the first Christian community in Jerusalem, we seek to imitate Christ through our unanimity.

This unanimity in the Lord is the raison d'être of all the other components, but being united as a community does not mean that everyone must always think the same way; unity does not mean conformity. As we grow in awareness and intensity of the love of God, we grow in love for one another, and that unity is what creates a harmonious environment. This self-offering is possible when charity grows within, and we are one in this purpose.

Charity in this context is not about generic kindness or giving money to the poor. Rather, as St. Thomas Aquinas notes, charity is friendship with God through grace — God giving us His own love, so that we might love with His own heart. Of course, God is transcendent and far beyond us, but He chose to become incarnate, taking on our human nature and uniting himself with us. Even now, He comes to dwell within us through grace, making us sharers in His life. Because of our friendship with Him, we can love those around us. This relationship with Him is our lifeblood.

How do we get to heaven? Partly by creating heaven on earth, within our community. By aiming at God, each of us becomes closer to each other. The *Catechism* states, "All Christians in any state or walk of life are called to the fullness of Christian life and to the perfection of charity" (2013). Scripture says the same thing about how all are called to holiness: "Be perfect, therefore, as your heavenly Father is perfect" (Mt 5:48). The answer is in that *Catechism* quote: It's all about charity — love of God and love of neighbor out of love for God.

Dorotheus of Gaza illustrates this truth excellently with the image of spokes in a wheel: "[This image] represents God as the center and the various ways of human life as the spokes. If the saints who desire to draw near to God move toward the center ... they draw nearer to one another — one to the other — as they draw nearer to God. The more they approach God, the more they approach one another."[2] As we move closer to God, we are helping each other to get closer to the center. No one can do it alone, so the people we live with are God's gift to us.

At certain times of the year, our backyard has many northern flickers.

This majestic bird, when sitting on a branch, is predominantly white and gray with black spots and a red dot on the head. It is a large, dull-looking bird — and don't the people we see every day sometimes take on that boring, black and white appearance? In flight, however, the flicker is a magnificent span of surprising, beautiful gold. The flicker in flight illustrates the working of grace in my sisters. I am often surprised by the sudden shining through of their dignity in unexpected moments. For example, one time some messy trash had leaked out of the bag and was getting everywhere. I have no idea what was in the trash bag, but to spare you the gross details, it was an incredibly smelly mess. Cleaning it up, I felt my stomach clench. The sister I was working with suddenly let loose a battle cry: "For the souls in purgatory!" Instantly, I was reminded of the purpose for which we do everything and was completely reinvigorated by her "golden" grace and encouragement.

## Reconciliation

Each time we pray the Lord's Prayer, we petition our Father to "forgive us our trespasses as we forgive those who trespass against us." This keeps us aware of our own need for mercy, and also of our need to show mercy to others. What's conditional is that we first show forgiveness, which is not always easy. However, this is what is asked of us, for Jesus said, "If you love those who love you, what reward do you have?" (Mt 5:46). Love is easy when we are loved and difficult when we are wronged — it's so hard to love those we may not especially like, those who persecute us, and even those who hate us. And isn't it true that the ones we love the most can often hurt us the most because their bite has the most sting? As the psalmist laments betrayal by a friend,

> It is not an enemy who taunts me —
> then I could bear it;
> it is not an adversary who deals
> insolently with me —
>   then I could hide from him.
> But it is you, my equal,
>   my companion, my familiar friend. (Psalm 55:12–14)

When love is challenging, we begin with trust in the Lord, as the psalm continues, "I utter my complaint and moan, and he will hear my voice" (Ps 55:17).

Years ago, a sister much older than I would check me with a "Yes, Mother," gently reminding me that I was telling her what to do. Her tone was not snarky or offended; it was a calm, sweet way of encouraging me to be less bossy, and it is a good example of merciful love.

Augustine's rule states, "You are to love one another with a spiritual rather than an earthly love" (RA ch. 6, par. 43). This spiritual love involves constantly forgiving from the heart and constantly asking forgiveness, because "love covers a multitude of sins" (1 Pt 4:8). This reconciliation means seeing beyond mistakes, seeing the person God loves, the one created in His image.

Saint Augustine further instructs us to be as quick to apologize as we were to make the injury (RA ch. 6, par. 42). Harsh words fly out of our mouths fueled by anger, so it's important to be just as speedy to say, "I'm sorry." This practice is *extremely* effective in repairing injury, whether in monastic families or your own. To apologize or say, "What I did was wrong," is humbling, but this practice is part of acknowledging an injustice, being stripped of self-love, and growing closer to God in the common goal of our life. It's difficult for all of us in life, yes, but "with God, nothing will be impossible" (Lk 1:37).

## Mercy

At a Dominican nun's clothing ceremony, and again at her First Profession and Solemn Profession, where she publicly declares her vows, the Prioress asks the sister, "What do you seek?" The simple yet profound reply is "God's mercy and yours."

Mercy implies a defect in the one receiving it — one that needs to be remedied. By putting the request of mercy in our mouths, the order wisely teaches us of our insufficiency, and the way in which the community is meant to make up for it. We have the individual assurance, that "God has dealt graciously with me" (Gn 33:11), so we must pass it on. We seek God's mercy on us and for the patience, forgiveness, and charity to live with those around us.

St. Thomas Aquinas defines mercy as "the compassion in our hearts for another person's misery, a compassion which drives us to do what we can to help him."[3] Saint Thomas's definition hits on the two aspects of mercy: "compassion in our hearts" (affective) and the "compassion which drives us to do what we can to help" (effective). The heart moved with pity is the affective aspect, the interior transformation; the compassionate action is the effective aspect, the external activity. This twofold action of compassion is what it means to ask for "God's mercy and yours."

I need mercy to love my neighbor despite my nature. An excerpt from St. Thérèse of Lisieux's autobiography illustrates this quite well:

> Another time, I was in the laundry doing the washing in front of a Sister who was throwing dirty water into my face every time she lifted the handkerchiefs to her bench; my first reaction was to draw back and wipe my face to show the Sister who was sprinkling me that she would do me a favor to be more careful. But I immediately thought I would be very foolish to refuse these treasures which were being given to me so generously, and I took care not to show my struggle. I put forth all my efforts to desire receiving very much this dirty water, and was so successful that in the end I had really taken a liking to this kind of aspersion, and I promised myself to return another time to this nice place where one receives so many treasures.[4]

We humans are often tempted to become focused on little annoyances around us, and we need prayer, reconciliation, struggle, and conversion so that through God's grace we may triumph in charity because "in all these things we are more than conquerors through him who loved us" (Rom 8:37). Saint Thérèse's experience of *leaning into* the annoyance is an essential lesson in transforming a natural irritation into, by God's grace, a supernatural treasure. Sanctifying the ordinary changes everything.

I often marvel at the fact that twenty or more women of varying ages and backgrounds can live together peacefully. For me this proves the grace

of Christ. I can't say every day is a perfect one, with complete harmony and peace, but simply asking for God's mercy and the mercy of my sisters — my family — implies that I know myself to be a sinner in need of mercy.

Our property has many pine trees, and we learn while watching these proud, complacent trees as they bend with the squalling winds. Their flexibility allows them to "lean into" a wind-tossed struggle, and this is a tremendous mercy. By contrast, the rigid, mighty oak does not bend with the wind or snow; when a heavy snowfall hits before it has lost its leaves, its branches do not fold to shake off the snow. They crack and break.

I once heard a priest counsel, "If you always resist an obstinate person, there is not just one obstinate person." Like the pine trees we must learn to bend, fold, and be flexible — learning mercy by peaceably letting go of our own entrenched opinions or the way we want things to be done.

We must show mercy to those around us. Not only *should* we, but we have the wonderful capacity to do so, as Jesus told us, "Blessed are the merciful, for they shall obtain mercy" (Mt 5:7). It is easy to love people in the abstract, but love must involve particulars. It can be easy to love "children" until you have a rampaging two-year-old screaming in front of you. Love for the "community" is easy until someone offends or misunderstands you.

This need for mercy in common life is equally true of family life and the workplace. Recognizing our own weakness (seeking "God's mercy and yours"), we are freed to recognize the need for mercy in others. When you start to see the person as reflecting the image of God, you can come to love her.

It boils down to a remembrance that every human being is made in God's image. As Graham Greene says in *The Power and the Glory*, "When you visualize a man or a woman carefully, you could always begin to feel pity — that was a quality God's image carried with it. When you saw the lines at the corners of the eyes, the shape of the mouth, how the hair grew, it was impossible to hate. Hate was just a failure of imagination."[5]

This is the reality of our life together. You get to know people so well, their strengths and weaknesses, that even when you see a fault, it becomes what it is, a singular act. Sometimes knowing the personal attributes and background of a specific sister makes it much easier to have compassion for her, and this idea is true for most people we meet. It is the person, the sister, made in the image and likeness of God, that you love.

Many saints had the habit of praising God for the good qualities or characteristics of others. What artist would not like to be praised for his works? How much more should we praise God for the wonderful image of Him we find in our neighbors![6]

Throughout my life, my biggest mistakes and darkest moments have often strengthened my faith because they made me realize how desperately I need God's love and mercy. God is always so generous. In Shakespeare's *Merchant of Venice*, Portia says to Shylock, "The quality of mercy is not strained. / It droppeth as the gentle rain from Heaven / Upon the place beneath. It is twice blessed: / It blesseth him who gives and him who takes."[7] We all need to stand under the rain of mercy; it is there we learn to be merciful and thus through mercy both the giver and the receiver are blessed. This mercy demands sincerity; it cannot be forced, tense, or done to be seen. Rather, it is honest compassion.

## Growth in Charity

Nuns are often asked, "What is the greatest blessing of religious life, of being here in the monastery?" The first answer is always "God!" The second: "the common life!"

In truth the common life is both the greatest blessing and also the greatest trial. One sister says, "Common life is like being married to twenty people at once, with thirty-five opinions!"

Like the Church (or every household), every community is made up of saints and sinners — we are all sinners trying to be saints. Living together constantly can generate much friction and many opportunities for growth, as any married couple can attest. Community life works like a rock tumbler. Rough rocks placed in a tumbler rub against each other; over time the friction smooths away all the rough edges. This is the purpose and effect of the common life. Only by naturally and honestly rubbing up against one another can we become more polished in holiness.

Fraternal correction is an important aspect of common life that works toward helping along that polish. Saint Augustine says, "Indeed yours is the greater blame if you allow your sisters to be lost through your silence when you are able to bring about their correction by your disclosure" (RA ch. 4, par. 26). Fraternal correction — to point out, usually for amendment, the errors or faults of someone — is a work of mercy, carried out with humility, prudence, and discretion (see LCM 5). Correction needs to be more of a help than a hindrance, and it cannot stem from one's own agenda.

Naturally, sometimes a person is not disposed to hear what needs to be said; there are times when I am not ready or willing to hear corrections. Other times, I am receptive and take the words to heart. Fraternal correction must come from a place of love, and it takes both humility and courage to be righteously honest with those we love the most. Then, even our weaknesses become strengths for building up the family.

Living in a community that is multicultural, multigenerational, multilingual, and has a diversity of personalities, intellectual gifts, natural talents, and likes and dislikes creates a strange and admirable beauty with natural frictions and gentle corrections that can build us up.

Here's a personal example of casual correction and encouragement. A few years ago, I had a day where nothing was going right — it felt like catastrophe and chaos were my only companions. I decided to go out for a brief walk in the backyard to calm down. My face must have revealed my inner turmoil, because another sister saw me, winked, and said, "All for Jesus." This simple reminder refocused the rest of my day. I had let my problems loom until they seemed enormous because I had lost sight of the one thing necessary.

Often, both the most encouraging words and the most crushing words I hear come from my sisters — sometimes even the same sister. Part of growing spiritually is realizing that many times, even in those challenging words, a truth is spoken, and if I receive that truth in humility, I can become more aware of a fault. We know that we are journeying together toward God, and it is love that brings us together. Despite so many obvious differences, we are family. Encountering our faults and sins in the spiritual life is like weeding the garden. I begin by pulling out the big weeds. This makes me more aware of the medium-sized weeds, which must be pulled up with their roots. Once those are removed, I become aware of all the tiny, annoying little weeds that seem to number in the millions.

Love is willing to be patient, kind, and forgiving, no matter what benefit or negative consequences it will suffer. Showing mercy to others can be as simple as a contagious smile or a companionable wink that says "I understand" and can lift spirits. Though it doesn't come naturally to me, when I make the effort to find something praiseworthy about my sisters, and communicate it to them, it really changes both our attitudes for the better. I am grateful and happy to see the joy that a simple compliment can bring.

This love for our neighbor finds its source in our love for God and His love for us. Ultimately, Christianity is an encounter with a *specific* person, the Lord Jesus Christ, and we spend our lives learning how to love Him.

In Gabrielle Bossis' work *HE and I*, the author recounts conversations she reportedly had with the Lord. Jesus speaks to her, saying, "Love never repeats, you know. ... Take care then to comfort Me, very simply: a glance, an inward smile, even a movement of pity for My sufferings, or a prayer for sinners." He continues with further specifics of easy ways we can love Him: "When you hold back a word, when you put on gentle manners, when you do something against your own will, when you humble yourself, when you forget a discourtesy, when you sacrifice a pleasure to help your neighbor. Everything for Me."[8]

We can love God by loving those around us. A concrete example of this comes once again from Saint Thérèse, who shares about her annoyance with a particular sister: "Not wishing to give in to the natural antipathy I was experiencing, I told myself that charity must not consist in feelings but in works; then I set myself to doing for this Sister what I would do for the person I loved the most."[9] This resolve brings the passions and emotions under rational thought, working toward the Christian goal of loving God and neighbor.

As Scripture says, "the aim of our charge is love that issues from a pure heart and a good conscience and sincere faith" (1 Tm 1:5). This purified love can require a deep discipline to curb the tongue or to forgive from the heart, or to assist a sister in need. In his classic little work *The Dominican Soul,* Fr. M. M. Philipon, OP, states, "The joy of a soul is measured by its love."[10]

Each day, God presents us with these little opportunities to grow in love for Him, which brings us joy. When I was a novice, we had an elderly sister who was living here on hospice. In the few months before she died, each of the novitiate sisters were assigned a day of the week to eat supper and talk with her. I admit that I was very intimidated at first, but I mustered up my courage and spent every Monday evening with her, listening to her stories, concerns, and wisdom. It immediately became a huge blessing for me, and I began to look forward to this weekly ritual. The time I spent with that sister was beneficial to both of us. She needed someone to show her compassion, and I needed to learn the valuable charity of listening.

Loving a sister who does something nice for me is easy (especially when she helps me with a burdensome task), but it can be more difficult to love her when she has been harsh toward me or has somehow wronged me. Yet this requirement to love is what Christ is asking of us, and this is how we grow to live out "God's mercy and yours." Love of its very nature is diffusive. It goes out of itself and gives all that it has. In *Les Misérables,* Jean Valjean reflects on the same idea of asking "God's mercy and yours" by saying, "The supreme happiness of life consists in the conviction that one is loved; loved for one's own sake — let us say rather, loved in spite of one's self."[11] How difficult it is to let yourself be loved as you are and to love others as they are!

## Radical Dependence on God

We Christians must acknowledge the reality of our wretched states while simultaneously being aware of God's incredible love for us; it is foundational to our spiritual growth that we "never despair of God's mercy."[12] Being in a religious community is a bit of a pressure cooker; living so close together, it's hard not to notice each other's sins and mistakes. And as people committed to being Christ-like, even small mistakes can seem like a big betrayal of our way of life, or a hypocrisy. We can feel that way about ourselves too. I've reacted to my own sins by thinking that I'm not good enough to be here — not holy enough to be a nun. This way of thinking can easily lead to a destructive, self-centered, downward spiral, but in a certain way, the thought is completely true, and God wants us to hear it and grow from this.

I cannot *save* myself; God alone accomplishes any and all the good work in me: "O LORD, you will ordain peace for us, / you have wrought for us all our works" (Is 26:12). I will never conquer my sins by my own trying — and I am *not* holy enough — but God is merciful, and Christ has set us free. The evil one often tries to discourage us so that we will disqualify ourselves of our calling. Again, we must call on "God's mercy and yours." As the psalmist says, "he delivered me, because he delighted in me" (Ps 18:19).

The point is not "I am a sinner. Woe is me!" The point is, I am a sinner who can return to God again and again, and his mercy will make something good of my weakness.

It is so very important to see ourselves as sinners, because that truth un-veils the wonder of it, that God reaches down to our level and raises us up. This comes across beautifully in Sigrid Undset's novel *Kristin Lavransdatter*. Toward the end of the trilogy, after a long and challenging life, Kristin reflects on her condition:

> God had held her fast in a covenant made for her without her knowl-edge by a love poured out upon her richly [and despite herself] this love had become part of her, had wrought in her like sunlight in the earth, had brought forth increase which not even the hottest flames or fleshly love nor its wildest bursts of wrath could lay waste wholly. A handmaiden of God she had been — a wayward, unruly servant, of-tenest an eye-servant in her prayers and faithless in her heart, slothful and neglectful, impatient under correction, but little constant in her deeds — yet had he held her fast in his service, and under the glittering

golden ring a mark had been set secretly upon her, showing she was His handmaid, owned by the Lord and King who was now coming, borne by the priest's anointed hands, to give her freedom and salvation.[13]

Our rebellious nature so often leads us to fall short of our capabilities, yet God in His infinite mercy does not hesitate to pull us up from the mire. His faithfulness and love continue to beckon us toward union. This beautiful passage conveys a profound message about how grace builds on nature and works in and through individuals. I love *Kristin Lavransdatter* because I can identify with the stupidity of the cycle of sin she's caught in and the incredible mercy that God shows to her. This passage shows the truth of the indelible baptismal mark left on her soul, which is also left on our souls, claiming us for Christ and imbuing us with sacramental graces. No matter how often we set off to the pigsty, God is always on the front porch waiting to welcome us home. Truly, He has claimed us, and despite our waywardness, if we acknowledge our sinfulness and repent, He welcomes us back.

This paradox of pursuing holiness amid the growing knowledge of our own deficiencies is part of our transformation as we nuns or layfolk increasingly accept that we are completely dependent on God's prevenient grace. The saints know much more profoundly than we do their own sinfulness, but it does not separate them from God but somehow draws them closer, because "his mercies never come to an end; / they are new every morning" (Lam 3:22–23).

The wonders God has done for us, and is constantly doing, are new every morning and always a beautiful mystery, even amidst trials and suffering. Therefore, "I will sing of your mercies, / O LORD, forever" (Ps 89:1). God is always providing for us through His steadfast love, and we have only to sing of the beauty of that reality. "As the eyes of a maid / to the hand of her mistress, / so our eyes look to the LORD our God, / till he have mercy upon us" (Ps 123:2). With the same eager expectation, we reach out to God like a beggar, expectantly hoping for mercy.

## Ongoing Conversion

St. Thomas Aquinas states that "inordinate love of self is the cause of every sin."[14] We desire a good thing, which might not actually be our highest good. God is love, so an ordered love is ordered to Him (unity), and a disordered love is breaking that relationship through sin (scattered, disunified, manipulative, controlling).

A sin is a thought, word, deed, or desire contrary to God's law. Augustine states it so well when he says, "For anyone who loves something else along with you, but does not love it for your sake, loves you less."[15] When we sin, we substitute a created good, or our own self-indulgence, for the love of God, our highest good.

Some spiritual authors describe every sin we commit as driving a nail into a board, and every time we are forgiven, the nail being pulled out. Even after forgiveness, the board is still full of holes, because these sins, while forgiven, have disturbed the order of justice. In Hebrew the word for sin is *cheit*, and in Greek it is *khata* or *hatta*, which means "missed mark." We miss the mark when we sin and fail to glorify God. Sin is in opposition to *quaerere Deum*, seeking God. Serious sin puts us on a path that leads away from God and toward misery. Yet, again, God is merciful and will take us back if we ardently seek Him, confessing our sins. Only reconciliation can restore order and harmony.

St. Catherine of Siena saw conversion — turning away from sin and toward God — as necessary for the reform of the Church. She held herself and her sins as responsible for the state of the Church. We would probably judge the sins of Saint Catherine as trivial venial sins (if even that), but she understood how any sinfulness in the Body of Christ becomes a leprosy afflicting the Church's mortal members. Knowing that many others were more sinful than she, Catherine could only judge herself and relate how the sins of any and all of the faithful impoverished the whole of Christendom. Everyone shares in the rewards of the saints and the guilt of the sinners. This is what it means to be connected in the Body of Christ: all the members function together, and we are either of "one mind and heart" or we are scattered, like limbs without a body.

I share the example of Saint Catherine because I suspect that there is a widespread misperception that we religious have secured our goodness simply by taking vows. It is quite the opposite! "It is a fearful thing to fall into the hands of the living God" (Heb 10:31). In a certain way, it is almost better to fall, and to know how much we cannot save ourselves, that we might cling to Him and to His mercy. Better to cling to acts of faith, hope, and charity, than to ever believe that we *deserve* the grace He gives us.

On the other hand, it is always better not to fall at all, or to be accountable for our sinfulness — the only thing that is truly ours to claim, for grace is the source of all our goodness and a gift from God. Thankfully, the Lord looks with mercy upon us as Saint Paul says, "For God has consigned all men to disobedience, that he may have mercy upon all" (Rom 11:32).

Writing this, I feel cut to the heart as I consider the goodness of God. How important it is to set the fear of God always before our eyes! This disposition is captured beautifully by a man whom Dante meets in *Purgatorio*: "Horrible were my sins, but infinite is the abiding Goodness which holds out its open arms to all who turn to it."[16]

We nuns can never despair of God's mercy (nor should anyone, ever); we

must also never become comfortable in our sins. The intensity of the religious life can be overwhelming if we take our focus off Christ crucified. At the same time, Christ crucified is the perfect image of God's love for us. God uses trials, temptations, struggles, and moments when we feel helpless, in order that we may cling even more fervently to Him and let Him pull us out of the miry pit, the place to which our sins have brought us. As the psalmist says, "Many are the afflictions of the righteous; / but the LORD delivers him out of them all" (Ps 34:19).

In our trials, we are ironically blessed by God's mercy, and we are even more blessed when we ourselves show mercy and others are blessed by it. This ongoing exchange shows that mercy has no favorites; like rain it falls on the good and the bad alike. In the Assumption, when Mary was taken up into heaven, we are reminded what it means to continually "remember the end of your life, / and then you will never sin" (Sir 7:36). Following her example, we ask God for the grace of a happy death and the actual grace to live each moment with that goal in mind.

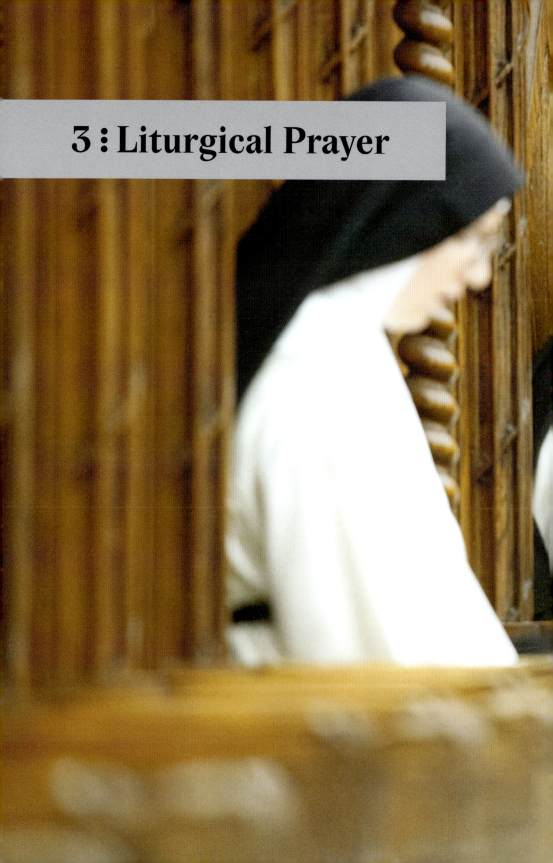

# 3 : Liturgical Prayer

•••

*O sing to the LORD a new song;*
*sing to the LORD, all the earth.*

*— Psalm 96:1*

•••

A little over fifty years ago, our monastery produced an attractive children's book about our life titled *The Golden Castle*. The castle is filled with princesses who come from all over the world to live together with the king and queen. Unlike most princesses, these women have no servants. Instead, the princesses themselves do all the work — cooking, cleaning, laundry, sewing, and making things to sell in the gift shop. But the most important work they do is talking to the king. Seven times every day they go to the "throne room" to adore the king, sing to Him, and keep Him company. There is even a special song for the Queen Mother that the king also loves. Anyone can sing this song, even if she doesn't have a good voice! When the princesses sing these songs, they ask the king to help the people who live outside the castle. The king and queen require no sleep, and they have a lot to attend to. But the princesses do need sleep, so they go to bed around 9:30. Still, every hour a princess gets up to go to the king in the throne room and keep Him company.

The "castle," of course, is our Dominican monastery, and the "princesses" are the nuns. Their main occupation — visiting the King, talking to Him, keeping Him company, and singing in His presence — is prayer. The saga ends with, "P.S. This isn't a fairy tale. This is a true story. I know it's true because I am one of the princesses who live in the castle at Springfield and Morris Avenues in Summit, N.J."

A Dominican nun's prayer can be either communal and public, or individual and private. "The King's Song" — when the nuns gather to praise God — is communal and public liturgical prayer.

Both liturgical and private prayer are complementary and mutually interdependent. The liturgy — whether the Mass or the Liturgy of the Hours — is intentionally set with periods of silence, which should be taken up in private prayer. At the same time, neither liturgical nor private prayer is really "private" because they are meant for the benefit of the whole people of God.

The ultimate goal of the spiritual life is the glory of God. The Second Vatican Council states that the primary purpose of liturgy is the glory of God and our sanctification, and notes that God is glorified precisely through our being sanctified.[1] Monastic life centers around the liturgy, continually returning to this most important work, over which nothing takes precedence.

## The Eucharist

*"Therefore, the whole life of the nuns is harmoniously ordered to preserving the continual remembrance of God. By the celebration of the Eucharist and the Divine Office, by reading and meditating on the Sacred Scriptures, by private prayer, vigils and intercessions they should strive to have the same mind as Christ Jesus." (LCM 74, IV)*

The Eucharist is the center of our lives, the center of the monastery, the climax of our day, the anticipated union to which we look forward, and the heart of our whole lives. The Mass is a full expression of what we as religious try to live all day: union with God, praise, sacrifice of our whole selves, intercessions, etc. In *Verbi Sponsa* we read, "Through prayer, especially the celebration of the liturgy, and their daily self-offering, [contemplative nuns] intercede for the whole people of God and unite themselves to Jesus Christ's thanksgiving to the Father."[2] Through our liturgical prayer we bring to Christ the needs of the whole world. "Consequently, [Jesus] is able for all time to save those who draw near to God through him, since he always lives to make intercession for them" (Heb 7:25).

The liturgy reminds us of the history of salvation, thus revealing the person and work of Christ. I like to think of tradition in the Church as a larger example of what happens in the monastery, where a story will be told again and again, until things that happened to sisters long past are told by current sisters as though they'd been there. Many here will tell you about our foundation day — how upon arriving at noon we ate ham sandwiches, pickles, and cake set on top of boxes. Of course, none of "us" were here on October 2, 1919, or even born yet! Yet this is "our" story. This living chronicle of the monastery, passed on orally from generation to generation, is like what happens in the liturgy when we hear the narrative of salvation again and again, until the stories become ours — our history and the record of our personal salvation.

Liturgical "memory" is different; rather than simply bringing a past event to mind, liturgical memory makes an event active, present, and powerful in our lives. In no sacrament is this representation as powerful as in the Mass, where the past event of Christ's salvific death on the Cross is made present to the Church and the world for the redemption of souls.

For us religious, the Mass contains a uniquely spousal dimension; we are offering to God the complete self-offering of Christ and making our own offering of self as well. The Eucharistic celebration reminds us to imitate Christ's self-sacrifice. Thus, by expressing the key elements of marriage — the self-gifting of spouse to spouse — the Mass contains the nuptial element, which is proper to all Christians but particularly lived and expressed by nuns, who are "hidden with Christ in God" (Col 3:3). As Saint Paul says in his letter to the Corinthians, "The unmarried woman or virgin is anxious about the affairs of the Lord, how to be holy in body and spirit" (1 Cor 7:34). The Mass focuses His handmaids on the Lord. In Holy Communion we receive and consume the Eucharistic Host — a most intimate moment whereby we assimilate our spousal Lord into ourselves. We consume and are consumed, uniting our hearts with His, seeking to be concerned only about the things of the Lord.

We live liturgically by matching our own fasting and feasting to the liturgical season. For instance, during Lent we enter into Christ's suffering and death through greater penances, including avoiding extras like dessert; in Easter, in the joy of the Resurrection, we "feast." Even our meals suit the season, overflowing from the liturgy into the food.

Each year, the cycle of Ordinary Time, Lent and Advent, Easter and Christmas, plays out and makes us ever more aware of the depths of Christ's love for us as we experience the mysteries anew. And this is not something exclusive to religious or clergy; all Christians can live out the liturgical year by using prayerful reminders — lighting the candles of the Advent wreath, erecting a Jesse Tree, displaying a desert icon in Lent, or enshrouding religious statues and artwork in purple during Holy Week; by celebrating the saints whose feast we remember daily and asking for their intercession, or finding all that is extraordinary, even in Ordinary Time, through simple devotions.

The Mass is perhaps the clearest touchpoint between consecrated and lay life. All participants unite on an equal field to share in the Eucharistic Banquet, joining their sacrifices in communion. You may ask, what is unique about this perspective, or what can your monastic experience teach me? *To be in His Presence!*

We believe in the corporeal, substantial presence of Christ in the Eucharist — Body, Blood, Soul, and Divinity. This is not just a symbolic or spiritual presence; Christ is *truly* present, himself. We are found in Him and He is in us.

We have all had the experience of being in the company of someone who was not truly present — someone physically there but distracted or walled-off. Sometimes we have been that person — I know I have, and more often than I'd like to admit. A nemesis of this deficient kind of "presence," Jesus is truly Present in the Blessed Sacrament in a way that surpasses any reality of how we are present to one another. In the Tabernacle, He is always there waiting for you and for me to make a visit, to sit before Him as He gives himself.

Jesus waits for us because He loves us. St. Thomas Aquinas states that the Eucharist is the greatest of all the sacraments, since only the Eucharist contains the substantial presence of Christ and His Sacrifice.[3] All the other sacraments are ordered to the Eucharist as their source and end. Jesus says,

"[Whoever] eats my flesh and drinks my blood has eternal life, and I will raise him on the last day ... He who eats my flesh and drinks my blood abides in me, and I in him" (Jn 6:54, 56). His Eucharistic presence transforms us, incrementally conforming us to His likeness. Our souls are filled with grace and a pledge of future glory is given to us (see LCM 75).[4]

In no other way can we Christians be more closely united with Our Lord — a union that extends beyond the communication of words, plunging into the very depths of our being. Christ instituted the Eucharist to be the sacrament by which He would continue to dwell with his disciples on earth, leaving a memorial and a testament to His loved ones: himself. Intimately united with Him in the Eucharist, the goal is to become Him, to continue to carry His presence within us and to each other throughout our days, to be ever mindful of His presence. And this is true for everyone. Even if you can only attend Mass on Sundays, unite yourself to Him spiritually every day through praise and prayer, seeking to carry His presence with you throughout your week.

One way contemplative nuns do this — and layfolk are encouraged to do it too, as possible — is by returning to His presence within the Liturgy of the Hours.

## The Divine Office (Liturgy of the Hours)

Whether prayed in private or as part of a religious community, the Divine Office, also called the Liturgy of the Hours, flows from the Eucharistic celebration as an extension of the Mass. Dominican nuns pray the same Liturgy of the Hours that is prayed daily by clergy, religious, and laity, establishing a universal bond of spiritual communion. The Eucharist and the Divine Office bring us into the compelling love of Christ; they set us on fire as we pray in the Psalms, "For God is king of all the earth; / sing praises with a psalm" (Ps 47:7).

The Divine Office sanctifies the day by celebrating the Word all throughout it via song, speech, and silence. Morning Prayer (Lauds) and Evening Prayer (Vespers) are the two "hinges" upon which the day turns, offering praise at sunrise for the beginning of a new day and thanksgiving at sunset for the many blessings found therein. Three times in between these hinges, recalling the customary practice of ancient Jews and early Christians, we pray again: at

nine o'clock (Terce), noon (Sext), and three o'clock in the afternoon (None). At some other time during the day or evening (it varies with communities) the Office of Readings is added, which includes longer scriptural passages and readings from early Church Fathers, Church documents, or other saints or writers. Our last formal prayer of the day is Compline, an office that has always been held in high esteem by the Dominican order. It is sung before the evening's silence with hopeful fervor as we recommend ourselves to the protection of the Blessed Virgin with the singing of the "Salve Regina" (LCM 81, III).

The whole of our lives is structured around this framework. We gather, chant the psalms, and attentively listen; the festal themes and readings provide a unity of reflection that flows into everything else we do. So, with "one heart and mind in God" we form a choir by every act of our day, which is sanctified hour by hour.

The psalms, which perfectly reflect the human condition in every age, also unite us with all humanity. In the chanting of the psalms especially, we mourn with those who are suffering, beg justice for those who are persecuted, and laud the peacemakers, the meek, the pure of heart, and the merciful. We hunger with those who hunger for God and continually thank God for His merciful love.

The psalms speak to the interiority of the soul, and they are constantly convicting me. Toward the beginning of Victor Hugo's novel *Les Misérables*, the good bishop decides to cross the mountains alone while notorious bands of robbers prowl the area. The townspeople, the mayor, and his sister worry about him. Upon returning two weeks later, he tells them, "Have no fear of robbers or murderers. Such dangers are without and are but petty. We should fear ourselves. Prejudices are the real robbers; vices the real murderers. The great dangers are within us. What matters it what threatens our heads or our purses? Let us think only of what threatens our souls."[5]

Sometimes the Liturgy of the Hours confronts us in this way, forcing us to examine the dangers within. The beauty of the psalms is that they not only express the depth of human emotion, but — hour by hour — they give expression to the afflictions of our hearts, forming us to acknowledge God's continual, loving providence. Saint Bernard expresses this in the spiritual context: "A brother's miseries are truly experienced only by one who has misery in his own heart."[6]

One of my great joys in praying the Divine Office is continually recalling the wonders God has done as the liturgical year rolls by and the pageant of salvation history is once more encountered. In his treatise *Against Heresies*, St. Irenaeus of Lyon reflects on the unending fidelity of God, saying, "He kept calling [his people] to what was primary by means of what was secondary, that is, through foreshadowings to the reality, through things of time to the things of eternity, through things of the flesh to the things of the spirit, through earthly things to the heavenly things."

The Liturgy focuses us on the eternal, for in a mysterious way, our whole life is a prolongation of the prayer of intercession of Christ. Our continual sacrifice of praise is offered in Christ, through Christ, with Christ, because such an undertaking could not be done in solitude or isolation. Augustine sums it up nicely: "Our thoughts in this present life ought to be centered in the life to come, and no one will be fit for that future life unless he or she is well practiced in the art of praising God now." We prepare for heaven by praising God *now*, recounting his past and present wonders.

The honest emotions within the psalms constantly bring me surprises, little treats, and even the occasional double-edged sword. I cannot count how many times I've gone to the Office feeling worn down and, sure enough, out of my mouth come the words, "Out of the depths I cry to you" (Ps 130:1), or "For you my soul is thirsting" (Ps 63:2, Grail), or "My one companion is darkness" (Ps 88:19, Grail). Other times, I've gone into choir feeling in awe of God, and we chant, "O give thanks to the Lord, for he is good, for his love endures forever" (Ps 136:1, Grail), or "I will praise the Lord all my days, make music to my God while I live" (Ps 146:1–2, Grail). Chanting the psalms plunges us into recognition of our human feelings, our faults and strengths, bringing us to deeper awareness of what it means to live out our calling as Christians.

Remarkably, praying the psalms seven times a day does not become boring over time; they remain ever new and exciting — like an eternal wellspring! We experience them, season to season, as fresh (because saying and hearing "I love you" is always new and precious and does not tire with repetition). We relish certain lines of the psalms and hold on to them, like dear friends, or we may have chanted a particular line a hundred times, but suddenly God gives us a grace of the moment to be caught up in it anew, and to ponder. This brings us fresh insight and growth in faith, hope, and charity every day. I chose Psalm 96:1 for the beginning of this chapter because the freshness of the psalms allows us to "sing to the LORD a new song," again and again. The wheel is not reinvented, yet our prayer is new, every day.

Can a kind of tediousness arise from our daily processions into choir and the pure routine of practicing prayer? Well, yes, but this sense of monotony, when it shows up, only calls us to go deeper — to fix our minds on God with a richer creativity, not that we may get something out of it, but that we may put something into it and be transformed by God's action, for His glory. This means renewing our attention to the pronunciation of words and their meanings, paying attention to what is prayed for, and, most importantly, courteous attention to God.[7]

For me, communal prayer never really becomes "old." Rather, it's like re-reading a novel like *The Lord of the Rings*. Each re-read brings a new discovery. In the Liturgy of the Hours, the Word of God spoken and sung becomes truly "living and active, sharper than any two-edged sword [and] ... discerning the thoughts and intentions of the heart" (Heb 4:12).

The living activity of the Word is a testament to the working of God in our lives now; and for us nuns, it is never boring. We are constantly being recreated, formed, shaped, and reshaped through it as God calls us, daily, to a new way of living, a new way of relating to Him and to those we encounter. Our prayer is experiential, not theoretical; it is alive, active, and recreative.

## Giving Glory to God

In mid-Lent during my postulant year, we began to prepare for Easter with chant practice almost every night. We went over all the Liturgies for Holy Week, the Easter Vigil, Easter day, and Easter week. Many of the pieces we only sing once a year, so we practiced hymns, responsorial psalms, the reproaches, responsories, the antiphons, and even learned new three-part, multi-page hymns.

One piece, meant to be the closing hymn of the Easter Vigil, was not well known by any of the sisters. We had to learn and build it note by note,

practicing almost every day until Holy Week. When the Easter Vigil rolled around, the Liturgy was gorgeous. At the close of Mass, our chaplain said, "Go in peace, alleluia! Alleluia!" and the nuns replied, "Thanks be to God! Alleluia! Alleluia," and then launched into the hymn. We were so well practiced that we knew every note, every breath, every change in dynamics.

You want to know the kicker? The doors to our public chapel were locked that night. The Easter Vigil is the only liturgy of the year during which they are locked, because for that celebration the lay people should be in their parishes, and monastics have no catechumens needing baptism or confirmation. So, that complicated hymn was sung so beautifully, solely for the glory of God! He knew how much we had practiced. He knew how much heart we put into praising Him. The purpose of the liturgy was perfectly served: to give glory to God.

# 4 : Dominican Prayer

•••

*Draw near to God, and he*
*will draw near to you.*

*— James 4:8*

•••

Saint Dominic did not leave his followers a method of prayer, or volumes of exhortations, or a technique for discernment. All he left us was his own example of prayer, which alone speaks volumes. Most of what we have is what was observed by brothers hiding in the chapel, spying on Dominic while he prayed. He was known to spend long nights in prayer, often making loud cries of supplication, gesturing as if having a conversation, listening, and using many bodily expressions of prayer. In his travels, preaching, teaching, conversations, illnesses, labors, he never forgot prayer.

The Gospels have many examples of the prayer of Jesus:

- Before He calls the apostles (Lk 6:12),
- When He heals the deaf mute (Mk 7:34),
- When He raises Lazarus (Jn 11:41–42),
- When He teaches the disciples how to pray (Lk 11:1),
- When He blesses the children (Mt 19:13), and many others.

Dominic imitated Jesus in constantly seeking God, retiring to a place of solitude for prayer (Lk 5:16), rising very early (Mk 1:35), or spending the night engaged in his orisons (Mt 14:23, Mk 6:46, Lk 6:12). Every day, wherever Dominic was, his thoughts were constantly returning to the Lord. Blessed Jordan of Saxony tells us, "[Dominic] gave the day to his neighbor, the nights to God."[1]

Dominic carried with him the Gospel of Saint Matthew and the Epistles of Saint Paul (and not pocket editions — medieval manuscripts, which were the size of an encyclopedia). So in love was Dominic with the Word, we are told he only spoke "with God or about God."

How can we imitate Dominic's example? Before seeking God, we must recognize that God has first loved us. St. Thomas Aquinas, in his *De Rationibus Fidei*, wrote this beautiful line: "Nothing can provoke love more than to know that one is loved." Knowing that we are loved makes it possible for us to love others. So the more we love God and seek His will, the more our union with Him and others is deepened or thickened, for love is a unitive force. Just as God has loved us, we are drawn to imitate Him by loving those around us; we grow closer to Him through those we serve. The twofold commandment, love of God and love of neighbor, is lived out in this way. "Therefore be imitators of God, as beloved children, and live in love, as Christ loved us" (Eph 5:1–2).

A wise elder Sister said to me once, "One can do incredible things, when one knows one is loved." Saint Bernard said something similar: "The more surely you know yourself loved, the easier you will find it to love in return."[2] Christ came to show us love, for He is love; this is the message of the images of the Crib and the Crucifix. God goes even further to extend His love for us through His abiding Presence in the Eucharist, the Sacrament of Love. Prayer is about abiding in that union, spending time with the One who loves us.

## Nine Ways of Prayer

Before covering private prayer and *Lectio Divina*, let's discuss Saint Dominic's Nine Ways of Prayer, written by an anonymous author between 1260 and 1288, probably at Bologna. These Nine Ways are a description of how Dominic prayed, in words and bearing, as observed by the brethren. These wonderfully physical medieval expressions of prayer illustrate the interconnection of the body and soul. Dominic used his postures to express his heart or even to groan loudly, and his example has permeated Dominican spirituality down the centuries. As we read in "Nine Ways of Prayer of St. Dominic":[3]

- The First Way of Prayer of Saint Dominic: *humbly bowing*. As we read in the Book of Judith, "The prayer of the humble and meek hath always pleased thee" (9:16, Douay-Rheims). Prayer begins with humility. Dominic taught the brethren to bow before a crucifix. In our monastery, we have the custom of kissing our scapular as a sign of remembrance of Christ who was humbled for us. Also, within the Liturgies we bow at the "Glory to the Father, and to the Son, and to the Holy Spirit."
- The Second Way of Prayer of Saint Dominic: *prostration*. As we read in Psalm 44:25, "Our soul is bowed down to the dust, / our body clings to the ground." Dominic would lie flat on the ground and cry, "God, be merciful to me, a sinner" (Lk 18:13). This attitude is a marvelous example of the disposition necessary for prayer, like a mendicant or a beggar coming before the Lord of All. By knowing the mercy of the Lord, we can be merciful to

others.

- The Third Way of Prayer of Saint Dominic: *taking the discipline*.
  Dominic would cry out, "thy discipline hath corrected me" (Ps
  17:36, Douay-Rheims). This penitential practice is offered for
  our sins or for those of others. Dominic was severe in his personal penances, but gentle and compassionate with others. He
  abstained from meat, observed fasts and periods of silence, selected the worst accommodations, the worst clothes, never allowed
  himself the luxury of a bed, all while continually praising God.
  These penances brought Dominic closer to God. We will examine penitential practices in a later chapter, but, taking this example of our founder, we see it here as a form of prayer.
- The Fourth Way of Prayer of Saint Dominic: *genuflecting*. Like
  the leper in the Gospel who knelt and said, "If you will, you can
  make me clean" (Mk 1:40), Dominic would kneel again and
  again, fixing his gaze on the crucifix. He would cry out with
  the words of Scripture, then attentively listen or speak from the

heart. Filled with joy, he would burst into tears with an intensity of desire "like a thirsty man coming to a spring of water." Here we again see an example and attitude of humility, confidence, conversation, and perseverance.

- The Fifth Way of Prayer of Saint Dominic: *standing erect on his feet*: "Our holy father Dominic would stand upright before the altar, unsupported by anything, with his whole body standing erect on his feet. Sometimes, he would hold his hands out, open, before his breast, like an open book, and then he would stand with great reverence and devotion as if he were reading in the presence of God." This is a beautiful example of conversational prayer. Dominic speaks, listens, ponders in his heart, savors the word of God, and takes delight in God's command. This example is not that different from the Divine Office, where we speak the Word of God, pause, and relish the words with a sort of rest and leisure, remembering them throughout the day. Even this liturgical action has a power of intercession.

- The Sixth Way of Prayer of Saint Dominic: *cruciform* (standing with arms spread out like a cross). Here the historical text reminds us of a great miracle of Dominic. Gutadona, a widow, had gone to the church of Saint Mark in Rome to hear Dominic preach and left her son, who was ill, at home. When she returned, she found that her son had died. Stricken with grief, she took his dead body back to the church. Dominic prayed with arms spread out just like Christ on the cross and stretched himself out over the boy's body, and he was revived.

- The Seventh Way of Prayer of Saint Dominic: *stretching*. We stretch our bodies up toward heaven in prayer, like a choice arrow shot straight up from a bow (see Is 49:2). In a way, this prayer elucidates the eschatological sign of religious life, prophetically pointing toward heaven. This is the dichotomy of the spiritual life: We are always one foot on earth and one foot in heaven, longing for heaven, but still living and working out our salvation on earth. Stretching upward is a reminder that our final goal is eternal beatitude, life with God. It is one thing to think, "I need to draw my mind to heaven," or even to just sit and think about wanting to be in heaven; but in my experience, this desire reaches a different depth when we involve our bodies.

- The Eighth Way of Prayer of Saint Dominic: *holy reading*. The text reads, "Sitting there quietly, he would open some book before him, arming himself first with the sign of the cross, and then he would read. And he would be moved in his mind as delightfully as if he heard the Lord speaking to him." As the psalmist says, "Let me hear what God the LORD will speak, / for he will speak peace to his people / to his saints, to those who turn to him in their hearts" (Ps 85:8). This way of prayer is tied to how Dominicans view study as a prayer with an alert, loving, and sober spirit, which we'll cover in a later chapter.

- The Ninth Way of Prayer of Saint Dominic: *praying while traveling or walking*. This is how Dominic used to pray, while walking with the brethren from one country to another, barefoot as was his custom. Sometimes going ahead, sometimes lagging, he would pray as he walked, and "a fire was kindled in his meditation." Frequently, he would make the sign of the cross. Even though we nuns are not traveling on foot from one country to another, we still "travel" around the monastery, and this is an excellent time to pray in this way. Like Dominic with his companions, we are traveling toward God like the spokes of a wheel, toward the center.

## Private Prayer

*"Prayer is the raising of one's mind and heart to God or the requesting of good things from God." (CCC 2559)*

Both liturgical and private prayer are important and necessary. I hesitate to use the word *private* because, while there is something personal about prayer, it is never an isolated affair. We always pray in Christ to the Father, because the Body belongs to the Head. Even our Constitutions state, "In the

midst of the Church [the nuns'] growth in charity is mysteriously fruitful for the growth of the people of God" (LCM 1, V). Prayer is our primary means for growing in charity and it becomes "mysteriously fruitful" because we are agents of the Holy Spirit, the Third Person of the Trinity. He desires to make known the love of the Father and the Son, abiding within us now and preparing us to know, love, and praise God forever in heaven. So prayer is transformative even though its effects may not be obvious. Sometimes we never learn whether prayers have been answered as hoped, but that does not mean that the prayer bore no fruit. Even if what we pray about does not transform a situation, it transforms us. Through prayer, we are changed — this is *always* true — and prayer has a positive ripple effect in the Body of Christ, the Church, for "where sin increased, grace abounded all the more" (Rom 5:20).

## Prayer as God's Gift

Prayer is our response of love to God's love. In the Gospel of Saint John, Mary of Bethany "took a pound of costly ointment of pure nard and anointed the feet of Jesus and wiped his feet with her hair.; the house was filled with the fragrance of the ointment" (Jn 12:3). Immediately, Judas objects, saying that the perfume could have been sold, with the money put to good use. This passage teaches us to see our time of prayer, passive or active, as part of a spiritual plan, not mere utilitarian action.

Prayer is God's gift to us, and often we do "waste" that gift, in the sense that we undervalue it, think it a task not worth our time. Neglecting prayer is in fact a grave waste because to pray is to love God and, as Mary demonstrates, love does not hold back, nor count the cost. In Matthew's Gospel, Jesus defends Mary, saying, "Wherever this gospel is preached in the whole world, what she has done will be told of in memory of her" (Mt 26:13).

Prayer is about "wasting" ourselves on Jesus. There is no place for meager utility in the spiritual life. Instead, it is always about love — seeking to love God as He has loved us and seeking to love one another as we have been loved. "In this is love, not that we loved God but that he loved us" (1 Jn 4:10).

Capturing the disposition of Mary of Bethany, John Cassian says that prayer is "first of all a plea for forgiveness and purity of heart. It is the cry of the sinner."[4] The cry of the sinner is not a morbid, "woe is me" but, rather, a total vulnerability and awareness of who we are as we stand before God. The plea for mercy is the beginning of the journey of prayer. After we acknowledge what we have done (and what we have failed to do), prayer becomes an expedition to follow Christ, who is always with us.

The opening line for the Office is the same cry of the sinner, "O God, come to my assistance ... Lord, make haste to help me," as is the *Kyrie* (Lord, have mercy) at the beginning of every Mass. We are always in need of His help. There will always be stumbling and a need for patience, but we can have courage because Jesus tells us, "In the world you have tribulation; but be of good cheer, I have overcome the world!" (Jn 16:33).

Mary anointed Jesus in complete humility which, paradoxically, is a by-product of prayer. David prayed, "Who am I, O Lord God ... that you have brought me thus far?" (2 Sm 7:18). In humble prayer, we realize our limited nature before the perfection of God to whom we are dependent for all our undertakings. We realize that of ourselves we can do nothing. As the character Christian in the allegory *Pilgrim's Progress* says, "That is that which I seek for, even to be rid of this heavy Burden; but get it off myself, I cannot: Nor is there a Man in our country, that can take it off my shoulders; therefore I am going this Way, as I told you, that I may be rid of my Burden."[5]

Our burdens are so heavy when we seek to carry them ourselves! Our lives become so much simpler, and lighter, when we recognize that we must yoke ourselves to Christ.

So many saints have helpfully defined prayer. St. Thérèse of Lisieux called it "a burst from my heart ... a simple glance thrown toward heaven." St. Teresa of Ávila called prayer "being on terms of friendship with God." For me, prayer is all those things, but it is also simply asking and thanking Him for what we are given, whether we receive what we asked for or not.

In prayer, the relationship of love is formed and sustained; even as we are always beginners in its practice, the very act of making this supernatural connection with our loving Creator draws us more and more deeply into God's strange, delightful, irresistible depths. We begin to see the awesome, tremendous love He has for us as His sons and daughters, and — as we bring our burdens into our prayer — we learn anew how deeply we depend upon Him.

Because God's mercies are renewed every morning (Lam 3:22–23), each morning deserves a fresh offering of praise and thanksgiving. As we need to hear that we are loved every day, so too we need to tell God that we love Him every day, in trust — bearing our intercessions and contrition throughout the day and into the evening. If we stumble, we get up and begin again. There is a continual looking forward to that merciful morning.

And none of this is unique to nuns; it's true for all who actively live the life of faith. Saint Augustine says, "God created us without us: but he did not will to save us without us" (see CCC 1847). We are responsible for doing all we can to conform ourselves to God's will, while simultaneously understanding that we are saved by God's grace alone.

## Prayer as Covenant

Just as the heart pumps blood to sustain the body, so prayer pumps blood into our spiritual life, sustaining our relationship with God. Prayer is relational and fosters charity, which is friendship with God. Pope Benedict XVI taught in his encyclical *Deus Caritas Est*, "Being Christian is not the result of an ethical choice or a lofty idea, but the encounter with an event, a person, which gives life a new horizon and a decisive direction."[6]

This is what it means to say the Word became Flesh. He desires union with us, by assuming our nature into His Person, fully God and fully man. He chose to implicate himself in our plight. Jesus is truly the Son of God, and it was for this identity that He was put to death. As the *Catechism* states, "The whole history of salvation is identical with the history of the way and the means by which the one true God, Father, Son and Holy Spirit, reveals himself to men and reconciles and unites with himself those who turn away from sin" (234). God desires union with each of us, and the whole chronology of salvation is ordered toward that end.

In the cloister, we feel keenly how God created us to give Him glory. Created in His image, we glorify Him when we reflect Him to the world and each other. Jesus has commanded us, "Love one another, even as I have loved you" (Jn 13:34). Our communion with Him is assured when we love those around us, helped by the sacramental and sanctifying grace of our baptisms, by which we are His children. Saint Thomas states that the smallest degree of sanctifying grace in one individual is greater than the natural good of the entire universe.[7] This grace makes us "partakers of the divine nature" (2 Pt 1:4), children of God, heirs of heaven, just and pleasing to God. It also gives us the indwelling of the Trinity, the capacity for supernatural merit and supernatural life (even raising us above the angelic plane). This does not mean our human nature is destroyed but — if we permit it and cooperate with God's grace — raised up and perfected.[8] This elevation of our nature through sanctifying grace is a totally gratuitous gift from God, a *conversio ad Deum* (turning toward God) to undo the sin of Adam.

The relationship we have with God because of sanctifying grace is a source of prayer. The *Catechism* tells us, "Christian prayer is a covenant relationship between God and man in Christ" (2564). The Holy Spirit, dwelling within, teaches us to pray.

A nun's entire life in community is a conformity to Christ Crucified. Our Constitutions say, "The whole life of the nuns is harmoniously ordered to pre-

serving the continual remembrance of God. ... Let Christ, who was fastened to the cross for all, be fast-knit to their hearts" (LCM 74, IV). Eating, sleeping, working, recreating, praying, are all lived as authentic moments of prayer, bringing us into union with God. Prayer is relationship, and growing in charity deepens our friendship with God; all moments that unite us with Christ deepen the friendship and increase our charity.

## Prayer as Communion

*"The life of prayer is the habit of being in the presence of the thrice-holy God and in communion with him." (CCC 2565)*

Imagine you had a boss who wanted to have a personal daily meeting at 9:00 a.m. Now, occasionally you show up at 9:00, sometimes 9:15, sometimes you leave early (with excuses), and sometimes you just don't show up at all. What do you think would happen, eventually? What do your actions say about your concern for your job, or your character?

Now, instead of a boss, imagine that you'd agreed to meet your friend or your spouse in the same way, only *they* were the unpredictable ones. Would you continue to show up when they are so unreliable? Relationships cannot flourish under these circumstances. In the cloister, we have the luxury of scheduled times of prayer, but the commitment is just as important for laity or priests. Everyone is called to be regular in prayer — committed — for this is how we learn to *want* to give our hearts to Him, to develop the relationship!

Every healthy relationship requires communication, which is simply heeding the Lord's invitation to sit at His feet and say what is in (or on) our heart. The apostles were with Him constantly, but it still took a long time for them to get that. Without daily, deep, intimate contact with Him, the relationship cannot grow; we cannot aspire to become like Him. And, as with any relationship, it takes patience, both with ourselves and with the Lord, who (one quickly learns) has a unique timetable.

The sacraments are like an intentional deep breath, a strong gust of wind filling our souls with a surge of grace, but our relationship with God is sustained by the life-breath of prayer. Prayer is not a mental checklist, either, where one decides, "I must say one Rosary, one hour of Adoration, three Aves for my children," etc. Rather, as Jesus is reported to have told Saint Gertrude, "A single word from the heart has far more power to free a soul than the recital of many prayers and psalms without devotion; the hands are cleaned better by a little water and much rubbing than by mere pouring a large quantity of water over them."[9]

How perfectly that captures the cleansing and purifying efficacy of prayer!

## *Lectio Divina*

In our monastery, private prayer consists in *lectio divina*, meditation, and study. In addition to this, our monastery has a special privilege and obligation to pray the Rosary in the presence of the Blessed Sacrament, taking half-hour turns throughout the day (except during the Office). We call this the "Hour of Guard." Other monasteries have adoration time or some equivalent.

*Lectio divina* is commonly understood as "spiritual reading," which over-simplifies this ancient mode of prayer. *Lectio divina* ("*lectio*" in brief) is part of our dialogue with God, as Saint Ambrose says: "We speak to God when we pray, we hear him when we read the divine sayings" (LCM 97, I). Or, as Pope Francis wrote in *Evangelii Gaudium*, *lectio* "consists of reading God's word in a moment of prayer and allowing it to enlighten and renew us."[10]

For *lectio*, the nuns primarily use Scripture, but other texts can be used as well. Four fluid parts make up the practice: First, in *lectio*, one reads slowly and thoroughly, seeking the meaning of the text. In *meditatio*, or meditation, one reflects, questions, and ponders over the text. In *oratio*, or prayer, one responds with praise, gratitude, repentance, or another surge of the heart for the Lord. Then, *contemplatio*, or contemplation, may flow out of the previous stages. Contemplation is a resting in the presence of the Lord. This is an action of God and is not something we can produce ourselves.

In his Commentary on the Creed, St. Thomas Aquinas gives a similar breakdown for attitudes toward the Word of God. First, we must *listen* to it, for hearing the Word gladly is a sign that we love God. Second, we must *believe* "that the Word of God dwells in us." Third, he recommends that "we should *meditate* often upon this; for otherwise we will not be benefited to the extent that such meditation is a great help against sin: your words have I hidden in my heart, that I may not sin against You" [Ps 119:11]. Fourth, we must *com-*

*municate* it to others: "one should communicate the word of God to others by advising, preaching and inflaming their hearts. ... Finally, we ought to put the word of God into *practice*: 'Be doers of the word and not hearers only, deceiving yourselves' [James 1:22]."[11]

I like to call *lectio* "marinating in the Word of God." It takes time and a continual soaking for us to be penetrated and tenderized, through a full immersion in these sacred texts. Pope Francis exhorts, "Never forget that 'the process of *lectio divina* is not concluded until it arrives at action (*actio*), which moves the believer to make his or her life a gift for others in charity.' In this way, it will produce abundant fruits along the path of conformation to Christ, the goal of our entire life."[12]

Blessed Jordan of Saxony described *lectio* thus: "Read over this Word in your heart, turn it over in your mind, let it be sweet as honey on your lips; ponder it, dwell on it, that it may dwell with you and in you for ever."[13]

In *lectio*, we may read attentively and be struck by a particular verse of Scripture or other reading, and we take this to be an invitation by the Holy Spirit to stop and ponder this phrase — to bring it into *lectio, meditatio, oratio,* and *contemplatio*, and come out the other side with a spiritually and personally valuable insight, or a deeper understanding of God or ourselves or others.

The human tendency to delude ourselves or to get around the rules or to be self-deceived is an additional reason why it is so important to spend time in prayer. The meek recognition of the work of God and our own unworthiness clears away the murk of self-defensive falsehoods and delusions we construct around our reasonings; it brings us into the light of understanding in deeper union with God. Prayer demands this ongoing purification which is preferable to living a selfish lie or operating from the falseness of self-deceit.

A word about distractions: *Everyone* has them, and they are part of being real and human. Sometimes it's hard to sit still and concentrate in silence for even one minute. Our society has formed us to be restless, worried, and easily sidetracked. The best advice about distraction in prayer is also the simplest: Just refocus. Redirect the errant thought back to God. Saint Teresa of Ávila tells a wonderful anecdote about this. After receiving Jesus in Holy Communion, she became distracted by the sad state of the sandals another sister wore. In characteristic fashion, Saint Teresa turned this distraction into a prayer, saying, "Look at that, see there, all these years and that's what I'm thinking of when I just received you into my heart!"[14] Meek with herself, acknowledging her fault, but not beating herself up over it or dwelling in self-loathing, she simply brings it back to Jesus.

Sometimes with *lectio*, what may *seem* like a distraction is actually God trying to tell us something or a way to bring God into some aspect of our hearts. Father Herbert McCabe, OP, said, "People on sinking ships do not complain of distractions during their prayer."[15] His point is to pray for what is authentically in your heart. If you are sinking on a ship, cry out to God to save your life, tell Him what you want! If you sit down to pray and start worrying about your kids, an appointment, lab results, a dreaded meeting, or whatever, be like Saint Teresa and turn it into an honest prayer.

## Intercessory Prayer

"Have no anxiety about anything, but in everything by prayer and supplication with thanksgiving let your requests be made known to God" (Phil 4:6). Intercessory prayer is the action of holding up a petition before God the Father on behalf of someone else. God's grace moves us to offer ourselves on behalf of others, sometimes like a libation being poured out (see 2 Tm 4:6). It can range from saying an Our Father or *Memorare* for this person or intention, or escalating to deeper prayer and fasting depending on the gravity of the intention and the zeal with which we've been inspired through God's grace.

Christ is the one Mediator between heaven and earth (see 1 Tm 2:5), so our prayers are always to the Father, through Him. Christ, said Saint Paul, "always lives to make intercession for [us]" (Heb 7:25). We act as "secondary mediators," extending Christ's role as Mediator. We have taken to heart the words Jesus tells us: Ask and you will receive (Jn 16:24), seek and you will find (Mt 7:7), knock and the door will be opened (Lk 11:9).

At her First Profession of vows, a sister receives the black veil and, while it is blessed, she is "recognized as a house of prayer ... and a temple of intercession for all people."[16] This has always struck me as fundamentally important in our life as Dominican nuns. What does it mean to be a house of prayer? What is a temple of intercession? In Scripture, God says, "for my house shall be called a house of prayer for all peoples" (Is 56:7). In the Mosaic Covenant the Temple became the physical location where God would listen to the pleas of His servants and of His people Israel, when they prayed toward this place (see 1 Kings 8). Throughout the Old Testament, "house" and "temple" are ordered to that which is consecrated and consequently at the service and intercession of God. With the coming of Christ in the Flesh, His Body is the Temple; we are joined to His Body through the Church. As consecrated brides of the Lord, we hold in our hearts a special meeting place where prayer intentions arise before the Lord like incense (Ps 141:2).

One of my sisters recently received a letter from a friend who volunteers with cancer patients. She asked prayers for a young man in his thirties with a wife and two kids, who had terminal brain cancer and only a month to live. This sister began to fervently pray that this young man would not only be cured, but in the next month would walk out of the hospital praying the Rosary ... and that's exactly what happened. God, in His mysterious designs, looked with favor on the petition of His handmaiden.

Our prayers are mysteriously fruitful. For this reason, it could be said that "if contemplatives are in a certain way in the heart of the world, still more so are they in the heart of the Church."[17] Dominican nuns, as women consecrated to God, have a special relationship to the Church, being set apart for this purpose. It means we are at the disposal of others. Our monastery is a haven to which anyone can come or write to request our prayers, and they will find listening hearts and remembrance in prayer.

This phrase "house of prayer" is rich in meaning and, not surprisingly, a similar one is used in the Bible: "Like living stones be yourselves built into a spiritual house, to be a holy priesthood, to offer spiritual sacrifices acceptable to God through Jesus Christ" (1 Pt 2:5). Again, in *Lumen Gentium:* "The baptized, by regeneration and the anointing of the Holy Spirit, are consecrated as a spiritual house and a holy priesthood."[18]

Isn't that marvelous? How often do you pray or make sacrifices for others? Although contemplative religious invest a lot of time in acting as mediators, praying for others is not something exclusive to nuns. All of us can take to heart Jesus' promises: Ask and you will receive (see Jn 16:24), seek and you will find (Mt 7:7), knock and the door will be opened (Lk 11:9).

This is work for all Christians! All baptized Christians are called upon to make intercessory prayers, looking to the interests of others (see CCC 2634–35). We do not belong only to ourselves; we belong to Christ.

## Ask, Seek, and Knock

Petitionary prayer is never useless, and so we *ask*. Like mendicant beggars, we come before the King bowed low and with a fervent heart, pleading for what is needed. Sometimes, a certain grace will be granted thanks to prayers raised in trust for this person or that situation specifically. Indeed, there have been miracles (praise God!).

Venerable Fulton Sheen poignantly said, "Ever since the days of Adam, man has been hiding from God and saying, 'God is hard to find.'"[19] Sometimes we pray blindly — like pilots flying on instruments — not knowing precisely what we are looking for or how to ask, yet still seeking God's will and favor. Our petitions do not try to *manipulate* God but, as St. Gregory the Great says, "By asking, men may deserve to receive what almighty God from eternity is disposed to give."[20] Through praying in this way, we share in the mystery of God's divine providence.

## Use Specifics

As with almost everything, with prayer you need to know what you are seeking before you set out to find it. Specific intentions and details are necessary. Sometimes I feel as if I carry around within me these dozens (or hundreds) of specific people and their intentions, echoing the beautiful words of Ruth, "Where you go, I will go, and where you lodge I will lodge" (Ru 1:16). Wherever I go, these intentions go, and wherever I am, they are with me in my heart. As a walking temple of intercession, this multitude of individuals are within my house of prayer, within my heart. "As a hen gathers her brood under her wings" (Mt 23:37), so these people or general intentions are gathered.

*Vultum Dei quaerere* boldly states, "The fate of humanity is decided by the prayerful hearts and uplifted hands of contemplative women."[21] From our relationship with God, through the baptismal priesthood, we pour out an offering of love, as a prophetic people of hope in faith to Christ the King. This relationship pivots on remaining in Christ: "If you abide in me, and my words abide in you, ask whatever you will, and it shall be done for you" (Jn 15:7).

Sometimes, however, even with devout and ardent prayer, it seems we do not receive what we have asked for. Because we are beggars, we leave every matter in God's hands, asking "Lord, be merciful" (Lk 18:13). We trust that He will answer our prayers with love and wisdom and "for welfare and not for evil" (Jer 29:11). Even Jesus reasonably asks what father, "if his son asks for a fish, will instead of a fish give him a serpent? ... How much more will the heavenly Father give the Holy Spirit to those who ask him!" (Lk 11:11, 13).

Understandably, when answers seem delayed or pleas denied, it can feel like our prayer is not being answered. It takes eyes of faith to wait patiently or to learn how to recognize the fish our heavenly Father provides. In this way, conversion is at the heart of every intercessory prayer.

Saint Paul says, "Faith is the assurance of things hoped for, the conviction of things not seen" (Heb 11:1). The conviction is constantly sustained by a sort of groping in the dark. Simply because something is not readily seen does not mean one stops trying to see it; we trust. We obediently hold that certain assurance of what is not seen.

What if the centurion of Matthew's Gospel, who sought healing for his servant, had doubted that Jesus could do it? What if he'd assumed the answer would be "no" (or didn't want to bother Jesus and just didn't ask)? A model of humility and the disposition of faith, the centurion approached Jesus confidently, asking boldly and specifically like a beggar, bringing empty hands to the King, who "is able to provide you with every blessing in abundance" (2 Cor 9:8).

Anyone and everyone has a "right" to ask for prayers, and we will wholeheartedly pass on these intentions to God. I have a special place in my heart for those who have tragically lost loved ones, women contemplating abortion, or priests who are struggling. Praying for priests is an intention dear to all monastic hearts because we know how much they need our prayers and of the widespread influence of good, faithful priests. Of course, every day we also pray for "generic" intentions, those that go unasked and are known only to God.

## Pray Always

Before entering the monastery, I gave a brief vocation talk to a confirmation class in Frontenac, Kansas. The teacher told the class, "After tonight, you will probably forget everything she said, but she will spend the rest of her life praying for you." It's true. The prayers are ongoing. Every Holy Week, I remember a man who tragically lost a son to a drug overdose after a long period of sobriety and always bring him and his family into my prayers.

Those who know Jesus instinctively turn to Him in times of need, great or small. Temporal needs are just as valid to pray about as anything, because prayer is about a loving relationship, trust, and asking good things from God (see CCC 2559). These "good things" include the mundane things of everyday life, for "when we share in God's saving love, we understand that *every need* can become the object of petition. Christ, who assumed all things in order to redeem all things, is glorified by what we ask the Father in his name" (CCC 2633). Whether praying for big things or little things, it all glorifies Christ.

Our community's motto is *Orate Semper,* "Pray Always." We see the words written in big letters outside our choir, reminding us of the needs of others each time we process through the doors throughout the day. We seek God who first seeks us, and we are called to be mediators of that seeking, "dedicating [ourselves] to Him with an undivided heart."[22] As *Verbi Sponsa* states, "cloistered nuns are ... a unique sign of the entire Christian community's intimate union with God. Through prayer, especially the celebration of the liturgy, and their daily self-offering, they intercede for the whole people of God and unite themselves to Jesus Christ's thanksgiving to the Father."[23] It's an incredible testimony to the faithful that they instantly recognize this sign and freely bring their intentions.

Recently, while I was teaching a class to the novitiate called "Theology of the Spiritual Life," someone brought up the slightly related topic of mystical gifts, especially bilocation. The youngest said she would love to have that gift so she could be in multiple places at once. Another sister said, "I don't think you get the gift so that you can do whatever you want. I think the Holy Spirit leads you." The discussion continued from the sublime to the more mundane as we noted that — while none of us have a glimmer of these gifts — everyone has a prayer life, and that certain intentions seem to hold more weight (or receive more attention) and thus become something we feel specifically led to pray for.

I concluded, "My mystical gift is that certain prayer intentions just 'stick'

to me when I hear them!" I find myself remembering them throughout the day — when I am praying the Rosary ("a guy I went to college with who is making unfortunate life choices"), or walking outside ("a woman in NY who loves to run and desperately needs God in her life, but is held back by the guilty weight of her sins"), or while cooking a common meal ("those who need jobs" or "those I know who work in restaurants"). The prayers arise all day long. Even years later, these intentions are still attached to me.

Truly, this is the missionary heart of a nun, embracing the whole world. Another sister told me that some prayer petitions keep her awake at night, echoing the cry of Dominic, "My God. My Mercy!"

There are always needs on our prayer request board, some urgent, some vague, some familiar; all of these we have promised to pray for — the discouraged, the wounded, those suffering from illnesses or dying, missionaries, the misunderstood, prisoners, priests, those facing difficult decisions, the unemployed, the conversion of a loved one, those struggling with a specific sin or addiction, and many others. All of us are constantly moved to compassion at these requests.

When I was a postulant, someone requested prayers for the family and friends of a twenty-four-year-old young man who took his own life. I remember his name and am still praying for his family and friends. I love, sometimes very deeply, the people that I remember in my prayers. St. Thomas Aquinas says, "And by the fact that anyone loves another, he wills good to that other. Thus he puts the other, as it were, in the place of himself; and regards the good done to him as done to himself."[24] With prayer requests, I pray for their temporal and spiritual good, and ultimately, I desire their highest good because I want to see them in heaven. We know that "those who seek the Lord lack no blessing" (Ps 34:10).

## Pray with Compassion

A moving passage from our Constitutions reads, "In the cloister the nuns devote themselves totally to God and perpetuate that singular gift which the blessed Father [Dominic] had of bearing sinners, the downtrodden and the afflicted in the inmost sanctuary of his compassion" (LCM 35, I). Separate from the world, but still part of it, monastic nuns take into our hearts the sufferings,

pains, and hopes of all peoples. Moved with compassion, Saint Dominic's plea becomes our own as we welcome all of those intentions into our hearts.

When someone asks for prayer, they are ultimately sharing a part of themselves, a deep part of their heart ("Pray for me, I am struggling with addiction," or "Pray for my sick mother!"). That takes humility and willing vulnerability, because it admits to fear (which too many mistake for weakness). By asking, though, we place a certain amount of trust in another, and ultimately in God, because we are letting go of the situation and trying to leave it in His hands, and that takes some strength, too. To paraphrase Saint Paul, when they are weak, then they are strong (see 2 Cor 12:10).

A doctor once asked me to pray for her self-confidence in her practice. Her humble request humbled me, too. Prayer requires a certain amount of purity of heart; it requires saying, "I know I can't do this on my own; can you please ask God to help me?" Breathtaking vulnerability! And a reminder that we are, mysteriously, all in this together.

Prayer requests come in all sorts of ways. A few years ago, I had a dream about a girl from grade school. I hadn't talked to or seen her for about fifteen years, but, taking the dream as a prompting of the Holy Spirit, I wrote down her name, praying for her good. Perhaps in that moment, she needed prayer. Also, about a month ago, I was praying fervently and impatiently for something to happen on a specific day, for a certain individual. Well, it didn't happen at all that day. Two weeks later, I had a humbling experience and almost immediately after, I got the good news that this intention which I'd prayed for had occurred. This succession of events was really a sneaky "God way" of answering my prayer in His own way and keeping me humble at the same time (and there really hadn't been anything "urgent" about the date, except that it would have been convenient for *me*).

Recently, I had an aggravating situation where I thought the answer had to be "A" or "B" and was praying to accept God's will in it. God pulled out a "Z" like a wild card — something I'd not even considered as an option. It was such a happy testament to Providence in how He designed it!

Often, we never know what happens when we follow these spiritual nudges of praying or doing for others. That's not important. At the end of time, we will be enlightened to see what it meant when we prayed for one another, and how the effect of our prayers have rippled through the years, impacting others, even other generations. Our hidden prayers, so full of grace, have the effect of permeating the Body of Christ, each prayer touching a soul, which then touches another soul. Knowing this alone should inspire us to grow in holiness. As the psalm prays, "Open the gates of holiness. I will enter and give thanks" (Ps 118:19, Grail).

Whether we learn the effects of our prayers in this life or the next, we continue to fervently make them, in hopes that all things are according to His purpose and plan.

## Remaining in Prayer

Private prayer is not restricted to a specific time but extends into a nun's daily activities. In commenting on 1 Thessalonians 5:17 ("pray without ceasing"), Augustine places a lot of emphasis on desire, or *concorditer,* the continual remembrance of God: "What does this mean if not: desire unceasingly the blessed life, which is nothing other than eternal life, from Him who alone can give it?"[25] This means whatever we are doing throughout the day, we can remain in constant communication with God, as this desire touches all aspects of our life.

Augustine also says, "Your desire is your prayer, and if your desire is continual, your prayer is continual."[26] Our desire is continually for the Lord, and everything we do should nourish that desire. Every step in following Christ is a step to fulfilling that desire, to praying without ceasing, and yet our desire for God also grows. "What else have I in heaven but you? Apart from you I want nothing on earth" (Ps 73:25, Grail).

# 5 : Evangelical Counsels

•••

*[Christ] humbled himself and became
obedient unto death — even death on a cross.*

*— Philippians 2:8*

•••

The three evangelical counsels — poverty, chastity, and obedience — are Christ's invitation to us to respond to the divine initiative of love as a foretaste of future glory. They are a call to perfection addressed to every Christian disciple, but they belong in a particular way to the religious state. By the counsels and their corresponding vows, religious men and women offer three distinct goods back to God: external goods through poverty, the goods of one's body through chastity, and the goods of one's soul through obedience. Lived prudentially with faith, the counsels remove whatever is incompatible with charity from our lives (see CCC 915, 1973).[1] Ultimately, fidelity to the counsels frees us to continue Christ's self-offering to the Father for the salvation of souls.

According to canon law, "A vow is a deliberate and free promise made to God concerning a possible and better good which must be fulfilled by reason of the virtue of religion" (Canon 1191.1). This definition, based on St. Thomas Aquinas, emphasizes that a vow is taken to fix the determination of the will in carrying out a good intention.[2] Taken as vows, the counsels begin a total holocaust of self-offering in conformity to Christ.[3]

To vow poverty, chastity, or obedience is always an option in the Christian life, not a command; but Saint Thomas shows that these three counsels are the quickest way to God because Christ has recommended them and "Christ is our wisest and greatest friend. Therefore His counsels are supremely useful and becoming."[4] Christian perfection consists in our growth in charity, which is brought about by conformity to the evangelical counsels as taught by Christ. Ultimately, the evangelical counsels are "an expression of the love of the Son for the Father in the unity of the Holy Spirit."[5]

Nuns of the Order of Preachers make profession into the hands of the prioress of the monastery, pledging to a whole way of life and promising obedience to "God and to blessed Mary and to blessed Dominic, and to the Master of the Order of Friars Preachers, and to you Sister N.N., prioress of this monastery of N.N., and to your successors, according to our Constitutions" (see LCM 157, I). Whereas some religious formulas explicitly speak all three vows (or sometimes even add a fourth), this single vow of obedience reasonably and rationally includes all three counsels and demonstrates just how God is rational. His eternal law is a participation in His rationality; there-

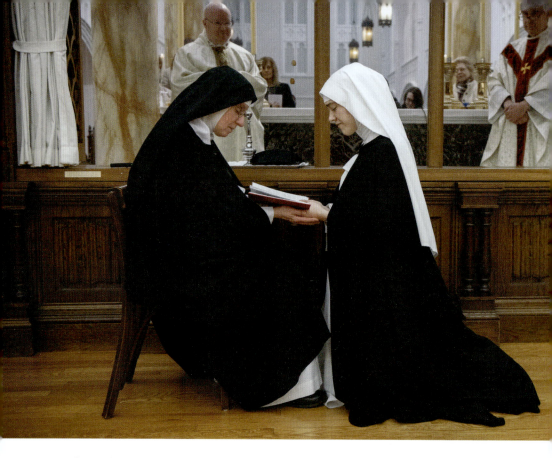

fore, *all reasonable laws followed are an act of obedience* for our good and the common good. This also means, concretely, obedience to God through the specific human being placed in charge of us: the superior or prioress.

Through this profession, practically speaking, we give up marriage, children, earning individual wages, and even the power to order our own lives. The promise of obedience to God, Mary, and Dominic is not a matter of justice, but of surrender, similar in a way to the self-offering in the sacrament of marriage. The commitment of love encompasses our entire way of life and dedication to spreading the Gospel through obedience. We vow ourselves to obedience in a surrender of love.

Obedience promotes the common good, which we should understand in light of the good of the Church and the order. On a practical level, if you are playing a game of soccer and everyone plays by the rules, then the game is much more enjoyable and in keeping with the final score. In the monastery, if everyone is obedient — playing by the rules, so to speak — then the final goal of the community can be more easily attained, and charity abounds.

Poverty, chastity, and obedience help us to fight against everything that may distract us from God. Like most rules or guidance, the counsels can seem hard and difficult to follow at first. However, with time, they become a beautiful way of life that gives us the freedom to follow Christ. The more you practice them, the more you realize the wisdom behind what previously seemed arbitrary. Like all virtues, they must be practiced constantly and continually stretched to grow in quality and be inspired by love.

## Obedience

Obedience, the most important counsel, teaches us to renounce attachment to our own will so that we may grow in charity. Jesus listened to the word of His Father to obediently do His will, and in the same way, we must deny our own will to do the will of the Father. Christ "emptied himself, taking the form of a servant" and "he humbled himself and became obedient unto death" (Phil 2:7–8). Obedience presupposes poverty and chastity, then obedience works to conform our wills and continues until death, just like Christ, our Exemplar. Saint Augustine describes obedience as "a disposition of the soul which governs all the attitudes of man so well that it is found at the root of all the other virtues and is also their crown."[6]

When I was a kid, my family sometimes went bowling, and we would always ask for the bumpers, which helped guide our wayward balls back to the center. Eventually, we developed enough skill to throw the ball down the center, outgrowing the needed assist. Obedience is like those bowling alley bumpers, except we *never* outgrow the need for it; we *never* develop enough "skill" to be perfectly conformed to Christ. While we live, we will always need assistance to guide us back toward Christ, our center. Sometimes I have been asked to do things I wanted to do and sometimes I've been asked to do something I didn't want to do, but responding in obedience to both has helped me grow as a person, a Christian, and a nun. Obedience is not about doing something out of fear or meeting the obligations of law. Rather, it is about letting go of selfishness (or fear, if we think ourselves unable to do the task) and conforming our wills to God.

Obedience brings all the other virtues together in love. Love must go out of itself to the object of its love. Dionysius, in *De Divinis Nominibus*, says, "Divine love causes a man to be out of himself, meaning thereby, that this love suffers him no longer to belong to himself but to Him whom he loves." The more we love God and seek His will, the more a relationship, and then a union, is formed. To freely vow one's obedience is to live out Christ's "not my will but yours be done" (Lk 22:42), or the beautiful words of Our Lady at the Annunciation, which we pray three times a day in the Angelus: "Behold, I am the handmaid of the Lord; let it be to me according to your word" (Lk 1:38).

All human beings are created to be free and, paradoxical as it may seem, submission through obedience can lead to freedom. Obedience is the opposite of slavery — rendered a deep and rich service because it's done entirely out of love. The commandments of the New Law are light to the one who carries them in love, and they are heavy when one tries to carry them without love.[7] As our Constitutions say: "Obedience, by which we 'conquer the deepest part of ourselves,' aids greatly in attaining that interior liberty which belongs to the children of God and disposes us to the free gift of ourselves in love" (LCM 19, III).

Christian obedience begins at baptism when we are incorporated into the death of Christ, who emptied himself. The more we respond freely to God's will, the more we are opened to receive His grace. As we grow in our religious formation, we discover that real obedience is not a suppression of the will, but rather a shifting toward God's will for us. Obedience to our superior shapes the unity that enables our common life, lived as one mind and heart, and following Christ. Any religious will tell you that of the three vows, obedience is the most challenging — the one that simultaneously bites the hardest and heals the most.

Our modern society teaches in various ways that for us to be happy, free, or successful, we must give free rein to every desire or whim of the will. Thus, it is radical, countercultural, and instinctually strange to want to freely give up your own will. Obviously, we do not *lose* our free will when we enter or profess the vow, but we *redirect* it. As a nun, there have been many things I didn't want to do, but I've done them (sometimes grudgingly) out of obedience and have been amazed at how cleverly God was instructing me in this way.

For example, I know of a sister in another monastery who did not know how to cook, not even how to boil an egg. She was assigned to the kitchen, and initially, her whole world was shut down: How could her superior ask this of her! Think of the poor community, suffering at her lack of skill! However, the grace of obedience unleashed in her a great humility to accept this job in trust. Initially, she relied on cookbooks and practical hints from other sisters, but with time she grew to love the work and became one of the most creative and skilled cooks in the community. Obedience led her away from her fear and allowed her to discover her own unplumbed depths.

It is important to remember that seeking the will of God must be the pre-occupation of both superiors and subjects. The superior can only command what is clearly spelled out in the law of God, universal law, or the proper law (the Constitutions of the community). Thus, not every wish or whim of the superior falls under the vow. Only formal precepts bind under the vow of obedience, given the explicit formula, *"I command you in virtue of the vow of obedience."* To not obey this command is extremely serious. However, as Our Lord says, "Whoever is faithful in a very little is faithful also in much; and whoever is dishonest in a very little is dishonest also in much" (Lk 16:10).

The promotion of the vow of obedience should be fostered through the cultivation of the virtue of obedience, which entails being faithful in small matters. For example, a superior could ask, "Could someone please volunteer to clear off the tables outside for the picnic?" and to follow this would be an act of the virtue. While we may not *want* to clean tables, this simple act of conforming our will cultivates the virtue of obedience. The perfection of the virtue raises the vow above compliance and conformity.

Unfortunately, the realm of virtue also leaves a lot of space for error and abuse, which is why understanding obedience and forming the conscience is so important.

Obedience is not meant to degrade or diminish the dignity of the human person; rather, obedience brings it to a maturity and freedom in charity.[8] Unless the action is evil or contrary to the laws of God or the Constitutions, we can be sure that our obedience to the superior is in fact the will of God. Then, there is joy and freedom in following God's will as the psalmist prays, "Your will is wonderful indeed; therefore I obey it" (Ps 119:127, Grail).

In the gift Mary made of herself to God, we see how obedience leads to love. As our Constitutions point out, "The vow of obedience is preeminent among the evangelical counsels, because by virtue of this vow, a person consecrates herself wholly to God; its acts approach more closely the goal of our profession, which is perfect love. By this vow, the nuns in their own way cooperate in the work of redemption" (LCM 19, I). In a particular way, at the Annunciation, and again at the foot of the Cross, Mary is the model of obedience. We seek to imitate Mary, who "through her obedience became a cause of salvation both to herself and to the whole human race."[9] Just like Mary, who lived in total obedience and self-offering to God, so the nuns desire to be always faithful to His will. The Constitutions later state that, "by our self-offering we may cooperate in the work of human regeneration" (LCM 24, I), which is firstly true of Mary, whose virginity was fruitful. The cooperative self-offering shows a fecundity linked to chastity. Just think of how many children Mary has fostered and nurtured throughout the centuries! Through our fruitful chastity, we too are fostering and nurturing souls for eternal life.

The prioress governs the monastery and, with the help of experience and a constant dependence upon the Holy Spirit, discerns what is most suited to the common good. In keeping with Dominican spirituality, the Constitutions explain, "The prioress ... 'should not take pleasure in ruling, but rather in serving all with charity,' and thus inspire in others willing service rather than servile subjection" (LCM 20, III). She leads by her example and is first among equals, following in the footsteps of Christ, who led by washing the feet of His disciples. I am always struck by the beautiful liturgy of the *Mandatum* on Holy Thursday, when the prioress takes up a pitcher and basin to wash the feet of each sister in the community. After washing, she gently kisses them — representative of the self-sacrificial service she offers in imitation of Christ. This aids our growth in charity, our following of Christ, and helps oppose the pull of the world and attachment to one's own will.

The vow of obedience gets at the center of the struggle within the human heart for our Creator. Loving God for His own sake is not easy for human beings due to original sin. Selfishness can always creep in. Thankfully, obedience is also not something we can accomplish on our own, otherwise the self would be inflated with more pride, right in the middle of trying to love. Two elements are needed: divine action (God's initiative of grace) and our response. God's grace does not force or do violence to our wills, but through time our wills can be conformed to His will. It is not an overnight, instantaneous project, but takes a lifetime.

## Chastity

In 2018, by a stroke of Divine Providence, we had the incorrupt heart of St. John Vianney here for a few hours as part of the "Heart of a Priest" tour sponsored by the Knights of Columbus. Venerating this relic of such a holy saint inspired me; this chaste priest had loved so deeply! While I prayed especially for priests, for the needs and intentions of the Church, and for the salvation of souls, this two-hundred-year-old little heart reminded me of a line we sing for First Vespers for the Solemnity of the Sacred Heart: "Deep in this Heart of His, the wound of love He bore."[10] The heart of St. John Vianney imitates the Heart of Christ, which we are all called to imitate.

The Gospel does not promise peace, security, and rest, but instead guarantees trials and temptations. Our sufferings, the wounding of our own

hearts, frees us to love as Psalm 66 describes, "we went through fire and through water, but then you brought us relief" (Grail). Only a heart purified through chastity can give love so freely to one's neighbors.

The second counsel, chastity, renounces the goods of the body, freeing us from disordered affections and subduing the interior impulse of the passions, i.e., lust. Chastity means the right use of human sexuality, and this right use is different depending on our state in life. It is Church teaching that Catholics are meant to renounce sex outside of sacramental marriage, and that her male and female religious must renounce marriage (in other words, be celibate). Chastity in marriage means the marital act, freed from lust and ordered to the good of the spouses and procreation. Continence — not using the sexual faculties — frees the disciple to concern himself with pleasing the Lord.

Chastity, which elevates bodily continence to a true virtue of the soul, is completely directed toward union with Christ in love. It frees us for self-gift, self-mastery, and self-possession, allowing us to be free to more fully love the other, "My belove is mine and I am his" (Song 2:16). Nuns, as brides of

Christ and consecrated women of undivided hearts, are concerned with the things of the Lord and pleasing Him (see 1 Cor 7:34). In marriage, love goes first to one's spouse and children; for the religious, the vow of chastity gives us the freedom to pour ourselves out in love for everyone.

"Truly God is good to the upright, / to those who are pure in heart" (Ps 73:1). Only the pure heart can see God because purity — an attachment to heavenly things and corresponding detachment from earthly ones — is required for love, if we are to meet with the All Pure.

Slaves to sin cannot be slaves of Christ. As the *Catechism* says, "There is no true freedom except in the service of what is good and just" (1733). Unless our passions are under control, we cannot attain higher levels of prayer in contemplation.[11] Sensibly, strong passions and external worries must be properly governed for a religious to do her work of contemplation, which is both an act of the intellect and the will. Thus, with an undivided heart, we seek to love God above all things and the world for His sake.

Especially in the initial stages, doing what is good can be genuinely difficult. One who grows in virtue becomes freer to do good. Eventually, someone can become so virtuous that it becomes easy, habitual, and indeed joyful to be good in almost any situation.

Perhaps to better understand the notion of "freedom" within chastity, we can think of someone who is overly fond of chocolate and finds it difficult to refuse it. The desire is so strong that — absent a helpful discipline — he or she does not in fact feel "free" to say no when chocolate is offered.

The freedom of chastity liberates us from the idea that we could ever save ourselves and thereby lifts the burden from our shoulders. Growing in love by the practice of the virtues helps us to grow in freedom. The more virtuous we are, the freer we are, that is, the more able to genuinely love.

Ven. Fulton Sheen wrote, "The Annunciation is the greatest act of freedom the world has ever known."[12] In her "yes" Mary was most free because she understood what God was asking of her and responded with grace. Although she could have said "no," as she had the perfect freedom to do so, her will was so aligned with God's that she wouldn't have done so. Grace builds on nature in the sense that, as she grew in grace, God's favor, her human nature was more perfected. Recall the words of Jesus in the parable of the talents, "For to all those who have, more will be given, and they will have an abundance; but from those who have nothing, even what they have will be taken away" (Mt 25:29), and the parallel line from the Magnificat, "he has filled the hungry with good things, / and sent the rich away empty" (Lk 1:53). Truly, Mary was "full of grace" because she continuously respond-ed affirmatively to the requests of God. She was completely free from fear. Her decision was not impulsive or hastily made; rather, she placed herself at God's service. Her will was free from attachments, free from acting through her passions, and free from the inclination to sin or concupiscence.

Saint Augustine categorizes freedom as an *intermediate* good, neither always good (like virtue) or always bad (like vice), but something in between, which can be used either for good or for evil. Ultimately, it is meant to be for good. One's freedom can be best gauged by one's aptitude to love. Chastity helps us unite ourselves to the chaste Christ so that we might love others rather than use them for our own pleasure.

One time we had a business transaction with a salesman named Antho-ny. In the course of our discussions, he looked at those sisters present with wide eyes, marveling, "You sisters are so pure of heart!" I suspect he wasn't responding to anything said by the sisters, but to the attitude with which we approached the transaction. I believe the virtue of chastity has given all of us a deep-seated purity that is radiantly different from most of the people that a salesman might deal with in his day-to-day.

Chastity is about freedom for love, not suffocating self-discipline. In *From the Depths of Our Hearts: Priesthood, Celibacy, and the Crisis of the Catholic Church,* which he coauthored with Pope Benedict XVI, Robert Cardinal Sarah reflected on chastity, writing, "How many times, while walk-ing for long hours between the villages [in Guinea, West Africa], with a brief-case-altar on my head, under the blazing sun, I myself experienced the joy of self-giving for the Church-Bride ... I felt quite palpably the joy of being entirely dedicated to God and available, given over to his people."[13]

While our roles are different, the Cardinal's joy for the Bride has been my own for Christ, the Bridegroom. The connection between chastity and purity of heart is everywhere because it is so essential. Christ does promise special blessings to those who have renounced marriage for the sake of the kingdom of heaven, saying, "Everyone who has given up houses or brothers or sisters or father or mother or children or lands for the sake of my name will receive a hundred times more and will inherit eternal life" (Mt 19:29).

Consecrated virginity and celibacy are about the kingdom of heaven. Religious men and women, as well as priests, stand as a reminder to our culture — an eschatological sign that points to God and the reality of things to come. Saint Cyprian wrote to the first Christian virgins, "You have begun to be what we shall be."[14]

Like all Christians, nuns can only live the vow of chastity by growing in friendship with God and relying on God's help. As the Constitutions say, "In their efforts to persevere faithfully and courageously in continence, the nuns will cultivate close communion with God through intimate friendship with Christ in all the circumstances of life. They should nourish this with the Sacred Scriptures and the Eucharist, and strengthen it by loving devotion to the Blessed Virgin Mary, Mother of God" (LCM 26, I).

Chastity most disposes one for contemplation, and contemplation disposes one for chastity. Aquinas distinguishes the difference between the exterior pleasure of carnal delights, which always leave us wanting more, versus the lasting interior delights of joy — when our hearts find rest in God. Of course, carnal pleasure is good when rightly ordered within the union of marriage, but often people use it to try to replace the joy that comes from God. If you have never tasted spiritual delights, you only delight in carnal pleasure, and when you have tasted the spiritual delights, you place them above the delights of the flesh.

Foregoing the delights of marriage does not mean that one cannot bear fruit. I remember my surprise the first time that I read 1 Timothy 2:15, that woman "will be saved through bearing children" (some translations read "childbirth" and some "motherhood"). Clearly, Saint Paul does not mean the more children you give birth to, the more likely you will be saved, for he goes on to say, "provided women persevere in faith and love and holiness, with self-control." Having pondered the verse, I believe he is speaking of physical or spiritual motherhood being a unique secondary way in which women work out their salvation, because Christ is always the primary means of salvation. Shortly before I entered, a friend's wife died after a brief illness.

Amidst the devastation and loss, someone begged me to spiritually adopt their three children, now motherless. Of course, I know they have a more powerful intercessor upstairs, but I faithfully and continually bring these three to God with me as I hold them in my chaste heart. As they grow, her children have drawn forth from me much willing sacrifice and love; they have no idea of their spiritual adoption, but I have not ceased to pour out my heart for them in tears, prayers, and sacrifice — a true effect of my chastity and a privilege of my vocation.

## Poverty

Entering the monastery as a postulant, I brought with me one black bag of the items on my clothing list: socks, white collared shirts, a Bible, a Rosary, toiletries for the postulancy, and so on. Nothing else. I had spent the months before that giving away items to friends and family, and even that morning I gave my coat away to a homeless man. As I crossed into the enclosure, I felt completely free. Seeking the treasure of heaven, I had sold or given away all my material possessions to follow Christ, trusting that God and the community would provide for all my needs.

The third counsel is for us to renounce attachment to temporal goods by embracing voluntary poverty. Involuntary poverty is an evil, because it is an (often unjust) deprivation of what humans need to sustain life. The poverty that Christ extolled was material and spiritual poverty, intentionally chosen. When done for love of God, this poverty can free us from our human and natural inclination to possess material things for oneself alone.

In the Gospels, when the rich young man asks Jesus what good he must do to inherit eternal life, Jesus replies, "If you would be perfect, go, sell what you possess and give to the poor, and you will have treasure in heaven; and come, follow me" (Mt 19:21). To be a disciple of Christ means we must first be detached from worldly goods, that we may be all the more dependent upon God. In this way, our charity or love of God grows as our relationship with Christ becomes our greatest possession.

"You cannot serve both God and mammon" (Mt 6:24). Poverty has different expressions, circumstances, and interpretations, even among religious understanding. Dominican poverty is in imitation of the Acts of the

Apostles, where all things are held in common and are at the service of the community. What material goods we possess together are meant to bring us closer to God.

Wealth can become an idol when we value its accumulation above the goods of heaven. It is a cruel master that never leaves one satisfied (see Eccl 5:10), and as Scripture says, "When your eyes light upon [wealth], it is gone; / for suddenly it takes to itself wings / flying like an eagle toward heaven" (Prv 23:5). The image of money sprouting wings and flying away from the one who pursues it is a perfect description of the empty rewards of making an idol of money. The more stuff you have, the more you must worry about the stuff you have. Alternately, when the rich give alms to the poor — when they act from Christian motives — they grow nearer to God.

The vow of poverty involves constant awareness checks to make sure we are not becoming too attached to our material goods or even turning them into idols. On a practical level, this means asking myself during my nightly examination of conscience, "Did I waste anything today? Was I a good steward of God's gifts? Did I have an inordinate attachment to something today?

Is this experience drawing me toward God or away?"

In a more abstract way, poverty can be about making sure we *love* the people around us and *use* the things — not use the people and love the things. Sister Seamstress is not just useful to me because she makes my habits, and I am not nice to her only because I'd like a new one. No. She is my sister, always.

One of my duties in the monastery involves woodworking. Perhaps Sister X asks to borrow a workshop tool that is in my charge and, through no intentional fault, she breaks it. It might be tempting to get annoyed with Sister X, but the fact that she had no intention of breaking it (and did not get hurt!) must come into play. Sister X is always much more important than the tools I use.

Our Lord blesses those who embrace poverty for the sake of the Kingdom, "Blessed are the poor in spirit, for theirs is the kingdom of heaven" (Mt 5:3). Poverty is not meant to be a destitution, but rather a freedom from attachment. People are *always* more important than material possessions. Material things, when shared, are divided; by contrast, spiritual things are multiplied by sharing. If I have a strawberry rhubarb pie and then divide it into eight slices among sisters, then each sister has one piece of pie, a part of the whole, and when eaten, it is gone. However, if I smile at, authentically compliment, or build up eight different sisters throughout my day, then (in theory!) this joy spreads, as they are in turn more pleasant to others. If everyone who reads the Gospel today with an open mind decides to be more charitable to just two people, the effect can be extrapolated dramatically.

Dominic sent out the brethren because he did not want the "grain to rot." The ideal of poverty of spirit is that all things come from God and, rightly, belong to God; as Saint Paul says, "What have you that you did not receive?" (1 Cor 4:7). We have received various gifts, graces, and blessings from God, and surely He too does not want us to let the good things he has given us — spiritual or material — to rot. We are meant to share them with others, trusting God to help the harvest increase hundredfold. When we hoard, oftentimes good things rot, both spiritually and materially.

On detachment from material goods, St. Thomas Aquinas writes, "[T]o attain eternal life, it is more useful to give up riches than to possess them; for those who possess wealth will with difficulty enter the kingdom of heaven, since it is difficult for one's affection not to be bound to the riches that one possesses."[15]

This sudden loss of earthly goods upon entering religious life (and occasionally later) can be a bit jarring. When I entered, I was shocked by how much I missed simple things I didn't expect to miss — playing baseball with nine skilled teammates, calling friends, eating out at restaurants, or even just using the internet. You don't realize just how attached you are to seemingly unimportant things until you must let go and feel the pain of loss. Some struggles you carry in your heart for a while, and others you just offer up to God and let go. Often, God surprises you by letting you enjoy snippets of them, like "monastery baseball," which is, in many ways, more enjoyable than a real game. Our version of baseball involves using about one hundred tennis balls and very creative pitching. This accounts for variations on the number of outs and how many times a person can bat. Usually, our best outfielder is the dog, who carries the ball away off the field (hence the need for so many balls).

On the other hand, upon entering I thought I'd never eat beef again or have a water-gun fight, which proved false (though it remains unlikely that I will ever ski again!).

More seriously, I know I will never have a biological family of my own, with all the human joys and opportunities for natural fulfillment it would bring. This is a loss, and all of us sisters must acknowledge this as we offer the possibility of physical parenthood back to God.

Still, as time goes on, an incredible freedom comes with not having to deal with material goods you seldom use or which do not enhance the quality of your life. Our Constitutions state, " 'We heed the words of the Lord, 'Go sell what you have and give to the poor and come, follow me' (Mt 19:21), and are determined to be poor in fact and in spirit" (LCM 28, 1, see Canon 600).

Poverty "in fact" and poverty "in spirit" complement each other and balance one another out. If the pendulum swings too far to the fact, it becomes a matter of legalistic accomplishment; if it swings too far to the spirit, there is no practical application. We need both to live poverty practically and spiritually, becoming poor in spirit in order to see the kingdom of God. The exterior practice and the interior application balance each other out.

For example, only having one outfit to wear every day (our habit), means not having to worry about what you are going to wear each day, or whether it is appropriate. Different communities have different practices, but for us only having two sets of sheets means we just swap them out and need not waste time thinking about the spares or where they are; one is on the bed and the other is in the closet or in the wash. Being satisfied with what is provided and not having to overthink simple things frees the mind to be able to just live.

Poverty also shows up in our talents or personalities. At Pentecost, the apostles were filled with the Holy Spirit. At our baptism, and again at confirmation, we are all gifted with the seven gifts of the Holy Spirit (wisdom, understanding, counsel, fortitude, knowledge, piety, and fear of the Lord) interiorly working in and through us. According to St. Thomas Aquinas, these supernatural helps are habits, instincts, or dispositions of the Holy Spirit that are necessary aids for us to attain our final beatitude: eternal life with God. Yet we are very different individuals. Some are skilled at art, science, singing, or speaking. Others draw stick figures or are tone deaf. Some are tall, some are short. Some are outgoing and bold; others are timid and shy. Some must work very hard at something while others seem like naturals. All these talents or "riches" are distributed differently in a community, and each is necessary for the building up of the Body of Christ.

The Constitutions say, "Community life requires a diversity of functions" (LCM 173), so each sister offers what she has in a spirit of service to the common good. The vows well-lived allow each of us to put these gifts at the disposal of the others, but this is not always easy. The life of a religious, in all her giftedness, is about giving life to herself and to others by generously giving of herself.

We all learn from one another. It is like each sister has an interior "treasure chest," which God has stocked with these talents to be placed at the service of the community. All day long we make withdrawals and deposits, large and small — a short sister in the kitchen may call out "Sister, you're tall!" In this sharing of gifts, the community is built up in love, boosted and enriched by this giving and taking.

It takes humility to accept (or even to ask for) help, to admit you can use a hand from your sister. Sometimes it is hard to convince an older nun to accept help from a younger sister; and at the same time, some younger sisters must learn the importance and the joy of looking out for the older sisters who need help and may never ask for it.

During my novitiate, we used to play a game in the backyard where we would go around and lift up heavy rocks and see what was beneath. Mostly we'd find the expected multi-legged creatures of God and occasionally, rarely, we would find treasures. The game was driven by the discovery of the Eastern red-back salamanders we'd unexpectedly unearth, beautiful creatures that no one here had ever seen before. Our spiritual poverty, which allows us to put all of ourselves at the disposal of others, can be like that game. Often, we expect a sister will be good at a certain task, and she exceeds our expectations. Other times, we expect someone will be bad at something, and she totally surprises us by having a hidden talent for the task. I'm so grateful for the unexpected treasures in the wonderful people God has created.

By giving of ourselves to the community in generous interdependence, we make a radical gift of ourselves, giving back to God what belongs to God. This way of living-by-giving actually encompasses obedience and chastity as well as poverty. Speaking of the sharing of gifts and the sense of belonging, Pope Francis in *Vultum Dei quaerere* says, "Only in this way can life in community provide its members with the mutual assistance needed to live their vocation to the full."[16] Intellectual talents, emotional finesse, acquired skills, and personality traits are all gifts that are our treasure to exchange for the greater glory of God. Let us be good distributors of the manifold gifts of God, and we will sing a new song of love.

Our Constitutions connect the vow of poverty with the Beatitudes, keeping our final Beatitude in mind, eternal happiness with God. It reads, "This spirit of poverty ... means freedom from enslavement to worldly affairs and even from anxiety about them so that we may bind ourselves more fully to God and devote ourselves more readily to him" (LCM 28, II).

Here we have the freedom that comes from the vow of poverty and what can be gained through all that is given up. Most people, including me, never realize how attached they are to "worldly affairs." It's human nature to want to know the latest news, what's happening, how so-and-so is doing, but such interests can be both enslaving and distracting.

The Constitutions continue, urging frugality. In a practical application, this could mean saying to yourself — "Today I will not use my computer" and seeing how attached I am to it, or "Today I will not check the mail" to examine how deep-seated my desire is to know. Detachment is an easy concept that can be surprisingly tricky in practice. When we are truly detached from goods, materials and even ideas, we may better enjoy the heavenly riches of God.

## Conclusion

All the baptized in every state of life (single, married, consecrated, ordained) are invited to walk this path of the evangelical counsels of poverty, chastity, and obedience, in imitation of Christ. The consecrated life, wherein the religious makes a public profession of vows and is dedicated to God for His honor and glory, builds upon the foundational consecration of baptism. Religious live out the evangelical counsels as vows, witnessing to the eschatological reality of the marriage of Christ and His Church.

This special bond with Christ means that religious also have a special bond with the Church. Poverty frees us from attachment to worldly goods, chastity frees us from attachment to bodily goods, and obedience frees us from the attachment to our own will. Jesus commands us, "Be perfect as your heavenly Father is perfect" (Mt 5:48), and these three ways are offered as a path to perfection.

# 6 : Hearing and Keeping the Word of God

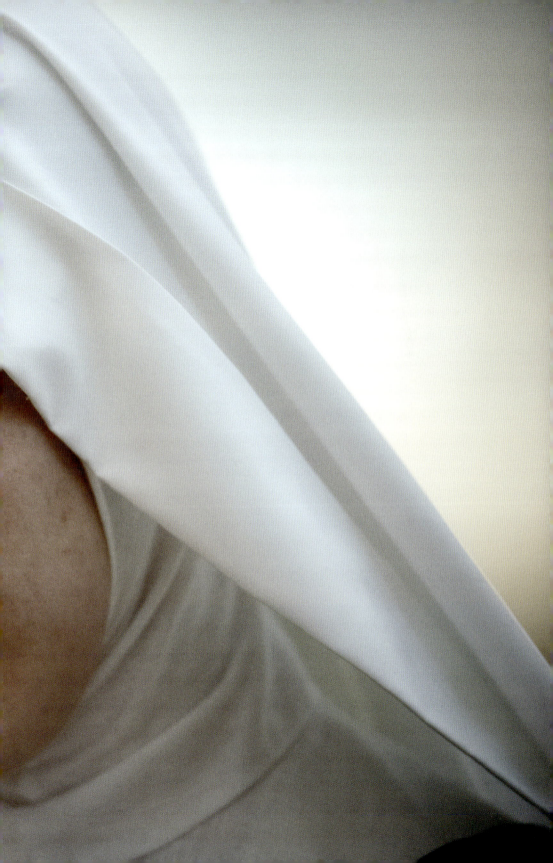

•••

*Your face, LORD, do I seek. Hide*
*not your face from me.*

*— Psalm 27:8–9*

•••

Saint Dominic, who had been a canon of the cathedral chapter in Osma, Spain, was asked one day to go on a visit through Southern France with his bishop. This area was ruled by the Albigensians, a heretical sect that held that there are two gods: one the god of goodness, light, truth, and spirit, and the other the god of evil, darkness, error, and matter. On their first night, Dominic and Bishop Diego stayed at an inn. As it turns out, the innkeeper was an Albigensian. Dominic engaged him in conversation, and the two stayed up all night talking. By the morning, the innkeeper had abandoned his errors for the truth, and Dominic had begun his preaching mission. Willing to take the necessary time and effort, Dominic showed this innkeeper the light of truth.

The Order of Preachers, *Ordo Praedicatorum*, was founded for "preaching and for the salvation of souls."[1] The nuns are associated with this "holy preaching" in a different way than the friars, Dominican laity, or active sisters. We preach by our prayer and penance, and we are reminded of our share in this mission every time we sign "O.P." after our names.

We spread the Gospel by offering ourselves to God. As the Constitutions state, "The nuns first build in their own monasteries the Church of God which they help to spread throughout the world by the offering of themselves. They accomplish this by being of one mind through obedience, bound together by love of things that are above (cf. Col. 3:1) through the discipline of chastity, and more closely dependent upon one another through poverty" (LCM 3, II).

Because we have no active apostolate, the nuns often appear "unproductive" — as seemingly useless as the perfume poured out by Mary when it could have been sold and the money given to the poor (see Jn 12:1–8). Some faithful Christians do understand and appreciate our mission, for which I am always very grateful, but our culture is losing its sense of the importance of religious women, especially contemplatives, dedicated entirely to God. Many want a utilitarian or pragmatic "need" for the nuns to exist, thinking that (just like the perfume) we *could* better serve by giving ourselves to the poor or "active" apostolic works. But whether we are cognizant of it or not, every human being's ultimate goal is the contemplation of God, face-to-face. The contemplative nun is already directly preparing herself for her chief act in heaven. Pope St. John Paul II in *Vita Consecrata* said it very well:

> Indeed, the life of cloistered nuns … "is nothing other than a journey to the heavenly Jerusalem and an anticipation of the eschatological Church immutable in its possession and contemplation of God." In the light of this vocation and ecclesial mission, the cloister responds to the need, felt as paramount, to be with the Lord. Choosing an enclosed space where they will live their lives, cloistered nuns share in Christ's emptying of himself by means of a radical poverty, expressed in their renunciation not only of things but also of "space," of contacts, of so many benefits of creation.

After emphasizing the sacrifice, John Paul turns to an explicit Eucharistic image of self-gift:

> This particular way of offering up the "body" allows [cloistered men and women] to enter more fully into the Eucharistic mystery. They offer themselves with Jesus for the world's salvation. … Accepted as a gift and chosen as a free response of love, the cloister is the place of spiritual communion with God and with the brethren, where the limitation of space and contacts works to the advantage of interiorizing Gospel values (cf. Jn 13:34; Mt 5:3, 8). … As an expression of pure love which is worth more than any work, the contemplative life generates an extraordinary apostolic and missionary effectiveness.[2]

While we do not engage in an "active" apostolate, this does not mean that we do nothing. As *Verbi Sponsa* states, "Cloistered contemplatives therefore are not asked to be involved in new forms of active presence, but to remain … dwelling at the very heart of the Church."[3] Monasticism, therefore, should be understood in this way: *Our very life* is an apostolate, an active and apostolic thirst for souls. Contemplative lives are dedicated to the very heart and soul of what drives all apostolic works: prayer and penance.

Our Constitutions state, "The purpose of all regular observance, especially enclosure and silence, is that the word of God may dwell abundantly in the monastery. Therefore, the nuns, after the example of the Precursor [John the Baptist], should prepare the way of the Lord in the desert by the witness of their prayer and penance" (LCM 96, II).

In imitation of St. John the Baptist, the nuns seek to prepare the way for God by our dedication to penance and the witness of our lives. These observances serve the purpose of making a fitting dwelling place for God's Word that we may (1) listen, (2) celebrate, and (3) keep the Word. This is how the Dominican nun remains with the Word, which is the intention of prayer, silence, enclosure, penance, and all regular observance.

All Christians can benefit from being reminded that prayer, everyone's intentional prayer, is the apostolate which supports every other good work.

## Listening to the Word

"Listen carefully, my child, to the master's instructions, and attend to them with the ear of your heart."[4] How important is that very first word of Saint Benedict's rule: *Listen*! How can any of us know what God is asking of us unless we first listen to what He has to say?

As nuns we *listen* to the Word in homilies; we *listen* while the other side of the choir is chanting the lines of the Office; we *listen* to the readings at Mass; we *listen* within *lectio*; we *listen* to the readings in the refectory; we *listen* to homilies and chapter talks.

We *listen,* but how much do we hear, so that we may understand what the Lord is saying to us?

In our modern world, listening to the Word and really hearing it is incredibly challenging. There are so many distractions constantly being thrown at us — so much noise taking up our internal bandwidth with emails, work obligations, and family activities — that our minds seem too roiled for simple acts of listening and hearing, especially when it comes to the stillness upon which the Word is breathed. Amid myriad distractions, how can we learn to listen?

Christ continually prayed and offered up supplication to His Father.

Imitating Dominic as he imitated Christ, we nuns are called to "perpetuate his 'fervor and spirit of prayer;' for 'he celebrated the whole Divine Office with great devotion;' 'was tireless in prayer;' 'during the night hours, no one was more constant in every way in prayer and vigils;' frequently 'he prayed to his Father with his door closed'" (LCM 74, III). This continual desire to be in communication with God and to foster a constant receptivity to the Word is at the heart of our following of Christ, in imitation of Saint Dominic. Jesus tells us "Pray always and not lose heart" (Lk 18:1).

On more than one occasion I have prayed and prayed, seeking out God for an answer to a question, and heard no response. I've been tireless, devoted, and constant; I've *listened* and yet heard nothing. When this happens, I become discouraged and sort of give up, trying to quiet down my own noise. Then, once patience has taken hold, the answer will usually come and I will "hear" it — through the Scriptures in the Liturgy, the Word in the refectory, or in a sister's casual observation. It arrives just like that still, small voice. As the Book Wisdom says, "Therefore set your desire on my words; / long for them and you will be instructed" (6:11).

God speaks his truth with us using multiple (sometimes confounding) means, voices, and expressions. Jesus, of course, is the primary revelation of God and the source of all truth. The revelation of God can also happen through "the book of nature" as well as through supernatural revelation (Scripture and Tradition). Then, through others we engage with, even a pagan philosopher, we have been given the ability to know the truth. God's truth is not limited to the wise or learned, and the Lord frequently makes use of unexpected people — for example, the prophecy of Caiaphas in John 11. So we dismiss the words of others — or listen poorly — at our own peril.

Several priests have told me that it is intimidating to preach to nuns because we are such attentive listeners. This observation follows the Thomistic maxim: *Quidquid recipitur ad modum recipientis recipitur*, which means "whatever is received into something is received according to the condition of the receiver."[5] When the preacher is preaching, the nuns listen closely because we are ready and eager to listen attentively to the preached word, and thus to receive in and through the Truth — the Word himself.

Remaining in the Word, we nuns hope to gain much from preaching and much from God, who does not disappoint us. As St. John of the Cross says, "we receive from God as much as we hope for."[6]

## Celebrating the Word

Celebrating the Word means really living it, according to the truth we have encountered. Once we encounter the Word, our lives are transformed. This is truly to live out the beatitude of the meek, to inherit the kingdom of heaven, which is within. Often the word *meekness* communicates weakness, low self-esteem, and being a pushover doormat, but this is not what Jesus meant. Instead, meekness is maintaining control in the face of difficult situations; it moderates anger with gentleness, caring, forgiveness, compassion, mercy, endurance, and calm.

Meekness is what Christ showed on the Cross: absolute power under control. To make yourself a home for the Word is to still go about your daily life with all its trials and persecutions and to show humility and acceptance when everything falls apart. As Jesus said, "Learn from me; for I

am meek and humble of heart" (Mt 11:29).

Living within the Word, we cannot help but be changed by what we've seen, touched, and heard. Everything mundane is brought into a whole new light of understanding by our encounter with God. What was dull now shines. We encounter the Word in the reading of the Scriptures, and our day is permeated with His Face. "Your face, LORD, do I seek. / Hide not your face from me" (Ps 27:8–9). We are not just reading words on a page but having an encounter with the Living God. Like a gentle breeze on a warm sunny day, you cannot "see" anything, but you know it is there.

The Greek word for "face" (*prosopon*) can also mean "person," "countenance," or "presence." The mystery of a person's face reveals their identity — who and (in a way) what they are. The Word is living and effective, transforming and changing its hearers. Human words fail to capture what is an experience beyond explanation. Shakespeare comes close in *Hamlet*: "There are more things in heaven and earth, Horatio, / Than are dreamt of in your philosophy."[7] Meeting the Word is supernatural. We can only get to know God by spending time in His Presence, listening and speaking.

Saint Paul exhorts us to "be filled with the Spirit, addressing one another in psalms and hymns and spiritual songs" (Eph 5:18–19). The communal gathering for the praying of the Divine Office is at the center of our lives, continually bringing our hearts back to God. In the psalms, Saint Athanasius writes that "the one who hears is deeply moved, as though he himself were speaking, and is affected by the words of the songs, as if they were his own song."[8] Sometimes, Saint Augustine teaches, Christ prays the words of the psalms as Head and sometimes Christ as Body. As "Body" all of our complaints, voices, and struggles, our anguish, our wrestling with God, and our hope are present in His praying.[9] The psalms are not just prayed as by individual subjects, but — as the Church Fathers understood — they are uttered in union with all, spanning throughout past, present, and future within the Body of Christ. When a postulant enters, we sing, "I rejoiced when I heard them say: / 'Let us go to God's house.' " (Ps 122:1, Grail) At a sister's funeral, we intone, "Give thanks to the Lord, for he is good; for his love endures forever! ... Open to me the gates of holiness: I will enter and give thanks" (Ps 118:1, 19, Grail).

Sung and chanted within the Liturgy of the Hours, the words of the psalms come out of my mouth with more expression and emotion than I would have given them on my own. Whether joy, sorrow, guilt, pain, or happiness, the Scriptures give perfect expression.

## Keeping the Word in Our Hearts

We monastics often hear, "What is the good of remaining locked up in that building for one's whole life when you could be out doing good for your brothers and sisters?" Honestly, the fruit of this apostolate is something that will only be known at the general judgment, when the events of human history become known to all. Moreover, it is worth pointing out that the keys are on the inside. Nobody is locked inside. The postulant's application is to get in (physical evaluation, psychological evaluation, autobiography, reference letters), not to get out. The monastery is a holy space, very hard to get in, yet easy to get out if one so desires. Instead, because we freely choose to live here in love, there is great joy and peace and growth in that as we seek union with God. As for the fruitfulness of our lives, we do know that "growth in charity is mysteriously fruitful for the growth of the people of God (LCM 1, V)." So, while we cannot immediately see the good or fruits of our prayers, this labor is not in vain as we mysteriously work to build up the Church. As Jesus says, "If a man loves me, he will keep my word, and my Father will love him, and we will come to him and make our home with him" (Jn 14:23).

This abiding in God is an abiding in love just as St. John of the Cross said: "At the evening of life, we shall be judged on our love" (CCC 1022). In the end, keeping God's word allows us to remain in Him, and from there we can truly love others.

Our Lord tells us, "Ask and it will be given you" (Mt 7:7, Lk 11:9) and "surrender to God, and he will do everything for you."[10] We have tremendous confidence that God hears our prayers and grants our petitions according to His own purposes. As the psalmist says, "Be still, and know that I am God" (Ps 46:10). We do not have to guess that the Almighty knows what He is doing; rather, we have a certainty that God is always working all things for good for those who love Him. As St. Thomas Aqui-

nas says, "Charity loves with greater fervor those who are united to us than those who are far removed."[11] We know that we cannot love in the generic sense; those who are closer to us or frequently ask our prayers are possibly more affected by our prayers, but, at the same time, prayer is not subject to relationship, proximity, or even time. Each prayer (and even every non-sinful action of a professed religious) is benefitting a particular individual or group of individuals, somewhere. This keeping of the Word is carried out in charity through prayer.

When Aquinas was still a young boy studying at Monte Cassino, he repeatedly asked the question, "What is God?" Sometimes our search for truth can seem like the thirteen-year-old boy seeking to know and love God, but the search must begin somewhere, and it is possible that Aquinas continued to ask this question and continued to find answers throughout his life. Our lives are a continuous study to understand what God has done for His people, from Adam until now, and what God has done and continues to do for us throughout our lives. You can't love what you do not know and so this lifelong study is essential to help us begin to know who He is (see CCC 236).

Whatever our state in life, we must continually ask God for the grace to *remain* faithful. The grace of perseverance is like the cry of the psalmist, "Remember not the sins of my youth, or my transgressions; / according to your mercy remember me, / for your goodness' sake, O LORD!" (Ps 25:7). We express a heartfelt cry of awareness of our frailty but also the unwavering hope that God remains faithful. It is because God has overlooked the sins of our youth that he calls us to follow him more closely.

In the Mystery of the Coronation (Mary is crowned Queen of Heaven and Earth), we are reminded of this wonderful example of perseverance. Parents do not dwell on every bad thing a child does while they are growing. They do not make a list and hold it against their adult kid for childhood disobediences. They forgive and love their children, always guiding them into further growth. How much more so does God forgive and love us?

During the ceremony for Solemn Profession, the prioress questions the sister about to make her vows, asking, "Do you wish to advance in the love of God and neighbor and to be truly a member of Christ, expending yourself entirely in winning souls, just as the Lord Jesus, the Savior of all, offered himself completely for our salvation?" To which the sister replies, "I do wish it, with the help of God, and yours." This response beautifully captures the spousal dimension of our vocation, completely offering ourselves to Christ. Then the Prioress questions her further, "Do you wish to be totally consecrated to God and dedicated to the universal Church in a new way, in order to announce prophetically the blessings of Christ and to enlarge the people of God with your hidden fecundity, and do you wish to be set aside for our order by solemn profession so that, while persevering in prayer with Mary the Mother of Jesus, you may ardently desire the fullness of the Spirit?" After the sister responds in the same way, the Prioress blesses this commitment: "May the Lord bring to perfection what he has begun."[12]

United to Christ, we take Mary for our model as virgin, bride, and mother. Her role in the Church is inseparable from her union with Christ and springs forth from it (see CCC 964). Mary is the model of faith and charity for every member of the Church, Christ's Body, listening, celebrating, and keeping the Word of God, but especially of religious women: "following in the footsteps of Mary, the New Eve, consecrated persons express their spiritual fruitfulness by becoming receptive to the Word."[13] We seek to imitate Mary in her fecundity by making a place in our hearts for the Word. She is the Queen of Apostles, the model of all apostolic works; she is our Mother Most Pure to whom we look as a model of purity of heart; and she is the Virgin Most Faithful in whom the evangelical counsels and beatitudes were completely incorporated into her manner of life. In the words of Pope Francis:

> From the annunciation to the resurrection, through the pilgrimage of faith that reached its climax at the foot of the cross, Mary persevered in contemplation of the mystery dwelling within her. ... Following Mary's example, the contemplative is a person centered in God and for whom God is the *unum necessarium*. ... Contemplatives appreciate the value of material things, yet these do not

steal their heart or cloud their mind; on the contrary, they serve as a ladder to ascend to God.[14]

Like Mary, we can hold the Word in our hearts, pondering what it means. By listening, celebrating, and keeping the Word, nuns "remain at the wellspring of Trinitarian communion"[15] and in a mysterious way, our prayers are fruitful for the building up of the Body of Christ.

In this chapter, I've focused on the life of the nuns, yet our relationship with the Word is by no means exclusive to the cloistered life. These same principles of listening, celebrating, and keeping the Word by setting aside daily time for reading, meditating, praying, and contemplating Christ apply to the lives of anyone serious about their faith. Saint Augustine defined virtue as "rightly ordered love,"[16] so by creating time and space in our hearts for the Lord, by perseverance in prayer, devotion to Mary, and speaking and living the truth, our very lives become ordered to God.

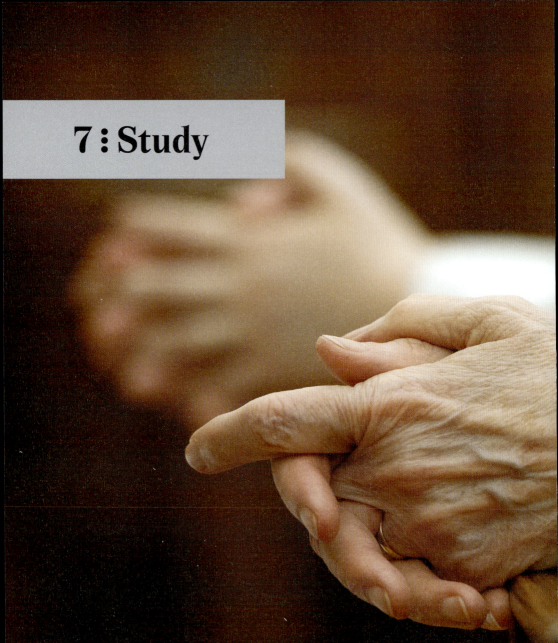

# 7 : Study

•••

*You will know the truth, and the*
*truth will make you free.*

*— John 8:32*

•••

Fresh out of the college setting, my understanding of study had necessarily been outcome-based: Get a good grade, pass the next test, produce the required paper, get a good job, and move along. In the monastery, study quickly became transformative: learning about God to love Him more. Study was no longer about acquiring information or satisfying curiosity, but rather about seeking union with the Truth, who is Christ.

Dominicans, especially Dominican nuns, seek to imitate Mary by holding all these things in our hearts and pondering them (see Lk 2:51). Through the years of initial formation — postulancy, novitiate, and first vows — we study specific subjects as well as our Constitutions, Augustine's Rule, and a wide variety of Church documents. Meanwhile, as a community we listen together to recordings or books during meals in the refectory, and as part of ongoing (lifelong) formation, we always continue to study, each according to our capacity.

The purpose of study is not to make a bunch of university professors out of nuns, but to prepare a home for the Word. When I strive to remember what I read and come back to reflect on it, the truth penetrates my heart and goes deeper than just making sure I read every word on a page. It becomes personal: "How does this affect me? What is the Holy Spirit trying to teach me through this passage?"

There are seven basic benefits of study as spelled out by our Constitutions. Study:

1. Nourishes contemplation,
2. Prepares us for *Lectio Divina*,
3. Aids human maturity and mental equilibrium,
4. Removes impediments which arise through ignorance,
5. Informs the practical judgment,
6. Helps us live the evangelical counsels better,
7. Constitutes a form of asceticism. (LCM 100, I–II)

There is a story of St. Thomas Aquinas being addressed by a voice from the crucifix, saying, "Thou hast written well of Me, Thomas. What reward shall I give thee for thy work?" Without missing a beat, Thomas responded,

"Nothing but thyself, O Lord!"[1] The brief dialogue speaks deeply about the formation and focal point of Saint Thomas's entire life of study. It is inextricably tied into the work of sanctification; our searching and knowledge should lead us to a deeper faith and love for the One we seek. God is the reward.

While we recognize that the most important aspect in the spiritual life is love, to be able to love, it is necessary to *know* those we love. Study and prayer, knowledge and love, are interconnected: one is constantly leading into the next. In her *Treatise on Divine Providence*, St. Catherine of Siena wrote to God: "You are a mystery as deep as the sea; the more I search, the more I find, and the more I find the more I search for you. But I can never be satisfied; what I receive will ever leave me desiring more."[2]

This truth is at the heart of the mystery of God: He cannot be exhausted. He is found and yet leaves us wanting more. When study is about the unfolding mystery of salvation, we have the promise that our search will not be in vain: "But from there you will seek the Lord your God, and you will find him, if you search after him with all your heart and with all your soul" (Dt 4:29). Whenever we spend time studying something, we learn and grow from our new understanding or the experience we've gained. This growth and transformation, in turn, further fuels our desire for study as we seek to follow Christ. This cyclical growth of knowledge and love continually impels us and transforms us into Christ.

Dominic was studying at Palencia when famine broke out in Spain in 1184. Throughout the towns, many were left hungry and destitute. He was so moved by compassion that he sold his most valuable possessions, his books, to provide provisions for the hungry. When asked about this, he said, "How can I study on dead skins, when live skins are dying of hunger?" Dominic loved his books and needed them; he was not simply memorizing information. Having books in his day was a luxury; since books were so valuable, it was, for him, like living with plenty in a world of poverty. So Dominic gave up his treasured possessions to serve the poor. If the goal of study is growth in love, we can conclude that Saint Dominic's study was not hindered but rather enhanced by the liquidation of his books, despite any material loss he incurred (easy access to texts and his own marginal notes).

Blessed Jordan shows us the wonderful interplay between study, prayer, memory, meditation, and works of charity as he shares that, while in Palencia, Dominic "began to develop a passionate appetite for God's words, finding them sweeter than honey to his mouth." He continues, "The truth which his ears received he stored away in the deepest recesses of his mind and guarded in his retentive memory. His natural abilities made it easy for him to take things in, and his love and piety fertilized whatever he learned, so that it brought forth in the form of saving works."[3]

Sacred study is for all Dominicans. For the friars, study is connected to preaching for the salvation of souls. They are to study the truth from diverse sources and on various topics, as a preparation for preaching. The Divine Office and even other religious observances can be dispensed at the discretion of the superior to give preference to study. Study refreshes the friar's knowledge and keeps his inner life young, zealous, and vigorous. The study of different fields of truth allows him to connect with others and bring souls to Christ. It receives nourishment from contemplation.

For Dominican nuns, however, study is about nourishing our life of contemplation and aiding *Lectio Divina*. Our whole life is harmoniously ordered to preserve the continual remembrance of God (see LCM 74, IV). Such a life, if faithfully lived, leads us to that perfect love of God and neighbor which is effective in caring for and obtaining the salvation of all people.

The connection between study and prayer is key to understanding its role. In fact, all elements of the Dominican monastic life are always working together and dependent upon one another. If one of the elements is lacking, the balance is off.

## Study Nourishes Contemplation

One of the mottos of the Dominican order is *Contemplari et contemplata aliis tradere*, meaning "to contemplate and to give to others the fruits of contemplation."[4] This phrase appears in the *Summa* and became a motto of the order because it links contemplation with the seemingly contradictory apostolic thrust of the Dominican mission. Saint Dominic stands as our model of how to bring together the active and contemplative lives. He shows us the intense life of prayer that goes together with engrossing study. Study is rooted in listening to the Scriptures and fidelity to the teaching and doctrine of the Church. As the psalmist proclaims, "I have sought you with all my heart ... I treasure your promise in my heart." (Ps 119:10–11, Grail)

More will be said on contemplation in a later chapter on recreation, but here we will show its connection to study, beginning with St. Thomas Aquinas's definition: Contemplation is a simple gazing at the truth.[5] He teaches that contemplation begins with wonder, an encounter with a good that our intellect must ponder. This means study should be something we cannot instantly understand.

Recall that truth is a conformity of our minds with reality, because truth cannot contradict truth. All reality is one, and our minds are made to know it by the power of human reason and faith. Faith and science or faith and reason are completely compatible and in harmony with one another. As Pope St. John Paul II said, "Faith and reason are like two wings on which the human spirit rises to the contemplation of truth; and God has placed in the human heart a desire to know the truth — in a word, to know himself — so that, by knowing and loving God, men and women may also come to the fullness of truth about themselves."[6] It comes from God and leads us back to God.

Study is where we open ourselves up to encounter this kind of Truth. It is not always easy, and it is not something that can be forced. This daily commitment makes it possible for God to allow us a "simple gaze at" the truth, be it through theological, philosophical, or mystical contemplation. This spark of wonder means a large part of contemplation is about *becoming aware* of what we do not know, like a beggar waiting for an insight. Sometimes it results in things we simply cannot express. It is not a static staring, but a dynamic engagement with the Indwelling Trinity.

Contemplation can be characterized as good, lovable, and delightful. In fact, Saint Thomas sees it as the purpose and goal of our entire life as human beings, a communication and sharing between friends.[7] Words are not always necessary. Though good, contemplation admits aspects of sorrow. Contemplation is a simple gazing at Christ, crucified and glorified, Truth itself. Every truth, whether natural or supernatural, comes from the First Truth, God himself. Therefore, our supreme happiness can be found in contemplating Christ crucified. Didn't Christ say, "When I am lifted up from the earth, I will draw all men to myself" (Jn 12:32)? This compelling wonder evoked by Truth, ultimately Christ, draws us to seek truth and find Truth.

When we encounter Truth, we are drawn to wonder (contemplation). In a way, study presupposes leisure, because reading and reflection go together. Intervals of time between periods of study or prayer are necessary for pondering over the truths we have encountered throughout the day. Leisure nurtures a capacity to receive reality, and study brings us into the truth of reality.

For anyone drawn to wonder and prayer, this is an important lesson. Often, after finishing a lengthy novel, intense movie, or detailed documentary, talking it over with others who have read or watched the same presentation can help us to unpack things we did not notice. In the way of contemplative study, giving our minds time away from reading words on a page allows us to "unpack" the depth of what is revealed.

## Study Prepares Us for *Lectio*

*Lectio divina*, the prayerful reading of Scripture, is intimately connected to study for Dominicans because it is ordained to a real dialogue with God. Study teaches us to focus and, yes, *unpack* the meaning of a text, which is the effect of *lectio*. We recognize in faith that the treasures hidden in the Word are inexhaustible, and we patiently unfold their meaning. Diligent dedication to study prepares our hearts to enter that sacred time of *lectio* eager to hear what the Lord God is speaking to us.

We bring into this fruitful prayer time of *lectio* all that we are, and it is important to be prepared — otherwise, it is almost like trying to cook when you do not know what ingredients you have in the kitchen. You can make a meal, but it might not be as good as it could be if you were prepared.

Study prepares our minds and our hearts, as well as our bodies, for *lectio*. The routine of consistently studying, every evening at the same time, habituates us for receptivity, by which we are nourished. Formed in this habit, sometimes our bodies are ready for *lectio* before we even notice the time. Our experience of studying at the feet of the masters and listening has us yearning to sit at the feet of the Master and listen.

To know God, and to understand the sacred Scriptures, we need to think correctly. Study is like the sharpening of a dull knife, honed so that it may quickly and effectively slice through to the good stuff. Scriptural commentaries, Church Fathers, historical backgrounds, St. Thomas Aquinas, critical exegesis — these all add great depth to our meditation by helping the story of salvation to come alive. So study becomes a preparatory work, taking us more deeply into the knowledge of love of God.

## Study Aids Human Maturity and Mental Equilibrium

Have you ever heard the phrase "making a mountain out of a molehill"? Sometimes, things in the cloister can become disproportionate, and the life can be a bit like living under a microscope. An unkind word can be mentally repeated and stew in our hearts. A misunderstanding can flare up, a disagreement can be brooded over for hours. I have found from experience that study cuts through a lot of the "swirl" that can go on in our heads. It enables us to "take every thought captive" (2 Cor 10:5). This involves bringing all our thoughts to Christ and in some cases dashing them against the Rock (from the Rule of Saint Benedict: "As soon as wrongful thoughts come into your heart, dash them against Christ").[8] We humans do have control over what we spend time thinking about and need to be diligent about redirecting bad thoughts and giving our minds good material to meditate on.

What we think about changes who we are. The imagination needs to be fed with good things, and we need at intervals to intentionally turn it back to God. It is crucial to continue to fill our imaginations and hearts with what we want more of in life: God. That's why the Scriptures are full of the best food for the imagination: "a feast of fat things, a feast of choice wines!" (Is 25:6).

Keeping a book journal is one practice that helps form my imagination and memory.[9] After I finish a book, I quickly pull out my journal and write out at least a page summary of the book, discussing things that struck me or an insight that I need to think about more. This has been useful in helping me figure out the meaning and purpose of the book I read. Sometimes, it is very personal: "This book pointed out how I need to work on custody of the eyes." (*Custodia occulorum*, or custody of the eyes, is a practice with a long history in the spiritual life. Practically, it means mortifying what you look at and guarding against curiosity.) Sometimes, it is very generic: "This book has an excellent section on the importance of prudence." This practice has proved extraordinarily helpful, not only for keeping track of books, but for retaining what I have read. Sometimes it can feel like a chore, but given how many times I have gone back to re-read summaries or recall insights, the practice is valuable.

Saint Albert the Great (1200–1280) was inspired to enter the order by the preaching of Blessed Jordan of Saxony. From his youth, he studied and observed everything in nature — fish, falcons, the moon and planets, plants and minerals — becoming the greatest naturalist of his time. Saint Albert interwove faith and reason, certain that science and theology were not at odds with each other because "the earth is the LORD's and all it holds, / the world and those who dwell in it" (Ps 24:1, NAB). In a similar way, any study we undertake gives us a knowledge of God, ourselves, the world we live in, the people around us. Studying the natural world helps us appreciate how the Word of God uses images in the natural world to describe God. Learning about creation helps us learn about the Creator. Healthy curiosity and wonder toward "the book of creation" can prepare us to wonder at the divine nature in a contemplative gaze.

Jesus used many examples from nature to explain what he was trying to teach — trees, beasts, birds, fish, farming, and other aspects of nature. Sometimes when we study these same aspects of nature, the context of His parables can come to life.

Because I love to work with my hands, I frequently study the mechanical aspects of design, construction, or machine and tool operations. On a practical level, this helps me with woodworking or fixing things around the monastery. At the same time, studying this area can be very good and "diverting" in a healthy sense for a contemplative nun. I also study a lot of moral theology, and sometimes picking up something lighter can help me to focus better. Another sister may love to study music or biology, and these diverse subjects help us to understand God, as we begin to see how intricately he designed everything.

## Study Removes Impediments Which Arise Through Ignorance

Sacred study removes impediments which arise through ignorance and informs the practical judgment. That sounds harsh, but really it is wonderfully helpful. Recall how Christ said, "I am the way, and the *truth*, and the life" (Jn 14:6, emphasis added). Sometimes, we misunderstand people or situations. Other times, we hold beliefs or ideas that are incorrect. Occasionally, our ignorance just leaves us in the dark. However, Christ, the light and truth of the world, has come to set us free from the bondage of ignorance and lies. Human beings naturally tend toward the truth and are obliged to direct their lives according to that truth (see CCC 2467).

Study is like rocket fuel in our search for the truth, and learning the truth about something where you were previously ignorant can be a tremendously freeing experience. Many of us have faced a temptation and thought, "If I just do it once, it will go away." We can rationally know that this thought is *not true* and yet still choose to follow the temptation. Studying morality in this context of seeking the higher good allows us to keep our end in mind while resisting the temptation, which brings victory. We quickly learn that fighting a temptation strengthens us in combat the next time the temptation comes around. Facing temptation is a bit like weeding the garden — if we allow the temptations to grow, they thrive. Instead, if we pluck them off when they are small, we give much more room for the flower (virtue) to grow.

We ourselves are the first beneficiaries of the discipline of study, as it greatly aids in clearing up our own ignorance first. This implies some action on our part, even if it only be a response to grace. We are called to study God's truth, to know God, and that same truth becomes exceptionally freeing. "You will know the truth, and the truth will make you free" (Jn 8:32).

## Study Informs the Practical Judgment

While the speculative intellect refers to that part of our intellectual capacity which recognizes truths for their own sake, the practical intellect applies such knowledge to action. The virtue of prudence perfects this capacity by which we know and choose rightly what the best course of action is in any given situation. Prudence is considered the highest of the acquired virtues because it has the widest application — it is the virtue that allows us to rightly pursue all the other virtues, properly directing their course.

Study helps inform the practical intellect and aids in the growth of prudence. This is about taking the things we learn and what we study and applying it to how we live. For example, knowing that "docility with respect to the advice of others" is an integral part of prudence can help us respect or even seek the advice of others when faced with a difficult situation.

Prudence takes the generic principles and applies them to specific situations, which is why it is both speculative and practical, an intellectual and moral virtue, involving the true and the good, both thought and action. Prudence has three acts or stages in its decision-making process: counsel, judgment, and command.

For example, if I see a cookie on the counter (counsel), I may decide that I want that cookie (judgment), and I consume it (command). Another way this scenario could play out would be that I see the cookie (counsel), decide that it is Lent and that I should offer it up (judgment), and walk away and say a prayer for priests (command). The second part of prudence, judgment, is where the practical judgment aspect of study fits in. An individual who is better informed through study makes better decisions and choices and, as a result, can have better actions.

## Study Helps Us Live the Evangelical Counsels Better

I was a little surprised to see in our Constitutions the connection between the evangelical counsels and study. However, I instantly agreed when I read it. Here's how poverty, chastity, and obedience relate to the practice of study.

### *Obedience*

Obedience comes from the Latin *ob-audire*, to "hear or listen to" (see CCC 144). Logically, you cannot be obedient to what you don't know or a command you've never heard. The more you acquire a habit of listening, the easier it is to obey. Study helps us to attune our ears to God. Saint Paul said, "Faith comes through hearing" (Rom 10:17). Truth is first heard and enters the ear before burrowing down to the soul where it takes root to transform through the Holy Spirit.

In 1211, a group of forty English pilgrims near Toulouse were on their way to visit the relics of Saint James in Compostela, Spain, but their small and overloaded boat flipped while crossing the river. Saint Dominic was praying in a church nearby and heard the screams. He responded immediately by prostrating himself in prayer. Then, as the cries of the pilgrims were lessening while they got further away, Dominic stood up and loudly said, "I command you in the name of the Lord Jesus Christ to come to the shore alive and unhurt!" At once the pilgrims were miraculously transported to the shore and safely rescued.

It was because of his attentive listening that Dominic was able to respond in prayers of intercession for the pilgrims. In the same way, sacred study is born from attentive listening. Because he was devoted to the Truth, throughout his whole life Dominic was able to listen constantly to what God was telling him, and he shaped his whole life around this "obedience to the truth" (1 Pt 1:22).

### *Chastity*

Study helps us to know Christ and His creation and therefore to love both better, and chastity is about loving Christ. Grace builds up a desire in us for the genuine good, and the effort put into study can contribute to the growth of this virtue. Knowing what genuine love is helps you to give yourself in love, purely, to those around you.

Saint Dominic confessed on his deathbed that he had taken pride in being able to preserve his chastity until death. He told his brethren, "God has in His mercy kept me till this day in pure and unblemished virginity." Then, he exhorted them to live likewise, adding, "I think I sinned in speaking aloud of my virginity; I should have been silent."[10] His admission was not actually a fault, just an honest revealing of the truth, since he clearly gave God all the credit, but it shows the necessary connection between chastity and knowledge of the truth. Saint Jerome said, "Direct both body and mind to the Lord, overcome wrath by patience, love the knowledge of scripture, and you will no longer love the sins of the flesh."[11]

Chastity helps us unite ourselves to the chaste Christ so that we might love others rather than use them for our own pleasure. It is totally oriented to union with Christ. We read in the Constitutions, "In practicing chastity we gradually and more effectively attain purity of heart, freedom of spirit, and depth of love. Consequently we achieve a greater control of mind and body, and a fuller development of our whole personality, by which we are enabled

to give ourselves up to God with greater energy, serenity and fruitfulness" (LCM 24, II). Dominic was well aware of this, and that is why in his last breaths he exhorted his followers to follow his example of purity of heart united with a search for truth.

## *Poverty*

In the sense that it requires being aware of how much we don't know (and how much we fall short), study springs from poverty and is itself a sort of poverty. As we pray in Psalm 73, "Whom have I in heaven but you?/ And there is nothing upon earth that I desire besides you" (v. 25). This relationship with God is the pearl of great price, and it is worth selling all you possess in order to have it.

One of the first "tools" that Dominic used to gain heretics back to the true faith was evangelical poverty. He realized that the ostentation and pomp of the bishops at the time — who seemed to place too much emphasis on worldly possessions and pleasures — were scaring souls away from the true faith. By living simply, practicing virtue, and living poverty, Dominic was able to reach the Albigensians, who believed that the material world was evil.

Saint Dominic was able to converse with the heretics because he lived what he studied, finding his treasure in freely choosing to go without. Poverty builds a bridge for study because we always stand as beggars before the Lord, and God provides. The study of sacred truth shows the spirit of mendicancy (begging). Study is a sort of training of our awareness both for knowledge and, simultaneously, for what we cannot know.

Dominic's joy was the seeming contradiction of "having nothing, and yet possessing everything" (2 Cor 6:10). His last will and testament says, "Behold my children, the heritage I leave you, guard humility, make your treasure out of voluntary poverty."

Poverty can evangelize, furthering the preaching mission of the order where words cannot, but it needs study to first know the sacred doctrine that can be preached. Dominic was truly a mendicant for the truth, always a beggar for the Lord and at the service of Truth.

## Study Is a Form of Asceticism

Christian asceticism simply refers to any practice of self-discipline or growth in the virtues for the purpose of union with God, and all the daily tasks of a nun's life contribute to this growth. From a personal perspective, the habit of practicing daily study as prayer is challenging. As Antonin-Gilbert Sertillanges, OP, states in his masterpiece, *The Intellectual Life*, "The great enemy of knowledge is our indolence; that native sloth which [will] make a big effort but soon relapses into careless automatism, regarding a vigorous and sustained impetus as a regular martyrdom."[12] The daily life of study is a regular martyrdom as our bodies protest and distractions become tempting.

The benefit of a daily commitment to prayer is like growing in any good habit. In the beginning, the gains are so small and often acquired through difficulty, but in the long term, it increases exponentially and forms the kind of person one becomes. It shapes our identity. Because of the little daily decision to study, one becomes the kind of person who studies and prays and, eventually — with commitment and God's grace — we defeat attachments to sins. And, if we continue to persevere in it, we reach the level of sanctity God desires for us. In the words of *Veritatis Splendor*, "in performing morally good acts, man strengthens, develops and consolidates within himself his likeness to God."[13] These small, good choices build on each other every day. Each good choice acclimates us to will the good and makes it easier to acquire good habits.

By contrast, think of a person who gets a sudden burst of energy and enthusiasm to clean her room. She goes all out, sweeping, vacuuming, setting everything to rights — she even makes her bed! However, after a few days, the books and papers start to accumulate in corners and on every flat surface. Two weeks after her cleaning spree, it looks just like it did before. Contrast that with the kind of person who spends five minutes a day keeping her room clean. Every morning, she makes her bed; when she finishes reading a book, she puts it back on the bookshelf. When she finishes reading or writing a letter, she puts it away. She has a neat, organized stack of papers that are at her disposal when necessary. Before she goes to bed at night, she checks to see if everything is organized and well-ordered, and she rests well knowing that she need not worry about where things are or what needs to be done.

I'd never tout myself as having the neatest cell in the monastery, but I've found that keeping it as organized and clean as possible helps me with the

rest of my duties. Doing "what should be done" every day is exactly how virtue works. The same applies to our daily practice of study, which trains us to persevere through something difficult for the mind. A random burst of energy for a running spree is sort of like the manifestation of curiosity (*curiositas*), and a regular routine embodies studiousness (*studiositas*).[14]

Saint Thomas noted that people have a natural curiosity for knowledge, but that curiosity must be governed by prudence and temperance, so he makes the distinction between *curiositas* and *studiositas*. It is no great thing to be interested in a whole bunch of different subjects without reason or focus — an important lesson today when answers to everything can be carried around in a smartphone. Curious information can sometimes become a distraction or so engaging that one forgets divine truths or seeks information beyond one's abilities and falls into error. There is also an important lesson in denying ourselves the constant gratification of harmless searching and curiosity. On the more mundane side, it can be a waste of time and energy. Studiousness, by contrast, is what we have covered in this chapter about being a lifelong learner, having discipline in our study of the truth, and allowing it to help us know and love God more.

Sacred study is about growing in love for God, not about acquiring academic degrees or reading many books to acquire lots of head knowledge. On this point Augustine was fond of quoting 1 Corinthians 8:1: "Knowledge puffs up, but love builds up."[15] Many other spiritual writers have warned sternly against this vanity or curiosity in acquiring knowledge.[16] We know that, "When he comes, the Spirit of truth, he will guide you to all truth" (Jn 16:13), so wisdom that springs forth from study is more than mere knowledge of facts. Like St. Albert the Great, we can increase our knowledge of God by studying books, using our senses, imagination, will, intellect, empirical data, and art, and by being attentive to those around us.

Spiritual study is meant for all Christians, and incorporating the action of daily study into your own life (even just ten or fifteen minutes before bedtime) can bear surprising, positive fruit throughout every aspect of your day. Study helps all of us to grow in knowledge of God, which helps us love the object of our knowledge more and brings us more intensely near to the One we love.

8 : Work

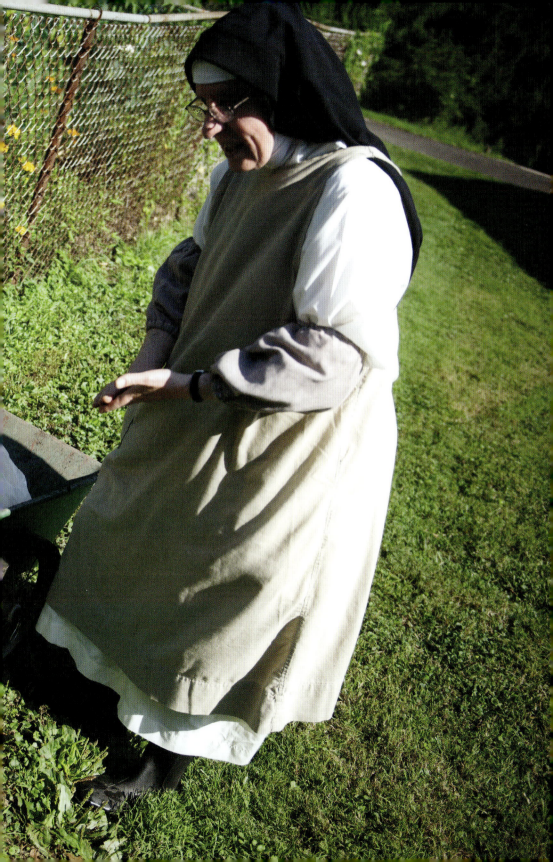

•••

*Whatever your task, work heartily, as serving the Lord and not men, knowing that from the Lord you will receive the inheritance as your reward; you are serving the Lord Christ.*

*— Colossians 3:23–24*

•••

According to tradition, Blessed Jane, the mother of Saint Dominic, had a dream before he was born. In this dream, she saw a dog leap from her womb and begin running throughout the world, lighting everything on fire with a torch it held in its mouth. She interpreted this dream to mean that Dominic would ignite the world on fire with sacred truth. Through the preaching and teaching of the Gospel, he would lead many to God.

This is the vision Dominic had for the order, and that same vigor for apostolic fruitfulness, conceived first in prayer, and the thirst for the salvation of souls born in love for the word of God, fuels everything we do. In a particular way, it determines what work we engage in and creates a spirituality of work that is rich in meaning. For Dominican nuns in particular, work incorporates many facets:

- Apostolic value
- A remedy for idleness
- A sharing and participation in the Creator's work
- Solidarity with the lot of many
- Another form of asceticism
- A fostering of unanimity
- A confident trust in the Providence of God

Just as Christ labored in His years on earth, we seek to follow His example.

Work has an apostolic value. We are laboring to build up and sustain the good of the monastery and simultaneously laboring to build up the kingdom of God. The work we do as consecrated handmaidens of the Lord is not an isolated undertaking solely for the purpose of having something to eat for dinner. Every human person needs to toil at some productive or operative activity for the working out of their salvation, including nuns! We work for the sake of growing in charity and being transformed into Christ.

On a practical level, work is a remedy for idleness — "the enemy of the soul and the mother and nurse of all vices" (LCM 103, 1). It allays concupiscence and prevents temptation. How many of us can say we did something stupid (or sinful) simply because of boredom? How many bad habits start because of boredom? Whether in a monastery or out in the world, we are all

the stewards of our time. Better to imitate God, who is pure act, and whose love "is never idle."[1]

There is a lovely story from the desert that relates the balance created by work and prayer. It seems some "men of prayer" approached an old monk, and the following conversation took place:

The old man asked them, saying: What work do you do with your hands? And they told him: We touch no kind of handiwork but, as the apostle says, we pray without ceasing. The old man said to them: And do you not eat? But they said: Yes, we do eat. The old man said to them: And when you eat, who prays for you? And he asked them again, saying: Do you not sleep? And they replied: We do sleep. And the old man said: And who prays for you while you are sleeping? And they were unable to answer him when he said this. And he said to them: Forgive me, brethren, but behold, you do not do as you said. But I shall show you how I pray without ceasing while working with my hands. For, with God's help, I sit down, steeping my few palm fronds, and from them I make a mat, while I say: Have mercy on me, O God, according to your great mercy, and according to the multitude of your mercies blot out my iniquity. And he asked them: Is that prayer or not? And they said to him: Yes, it is. And he said: When I have spent the whole day at work, praying in my heart or with my lips, I earn about sixteen coins, and I put two of them at my door and I eat with what remains. Whoever finds these two denarii prays for me while I am eating or sleeping, and thus by the grace of God there is fulfilled in me what is written: Pray without ceasing.[2]

There exists beautiful theology behind the statement that work is a sharing or a participation in the work of the Creator. We do not achieve creation but rather fulfill the Creator's plan, as we are "associated with the work of the Redeemer." The Constitutions say, "The nuns should readily give themselves to work with all their powers of mind and heart as well as their gifts of nature and grace" (LCM 104). So, as for all human beings, this work we partake in connects us with our Creator who is continually working in us.

As cloistered nuns are only indirectly involved in any apostolate, our prayers offered while working are important and efficacious for the salvation of souls.[3] These times of silence and attention humble us and unite us with God, which is mysteriously potent for the Body of Christ. Nuns do not need apostolic activity, because they seek the one thing necessary and are occupied with things that are above: Their contemplative life is their apostolate.[4]

In Leo Tolstoy's *Anna Karenina*, the character Levin, a nobleman, breaks social norms and works alongside his peasant servants in the field: "The longer Levin mowed, the oftener he felt the moments of oblivion when his arms no longer seemed to swing the scythe, but the scythe itself his whole body, so conscious and full of life; and as if by magic, regular and definitely without a thought being given to it, the work accomplished itself of its own accord. These were blessed moments."[5] Levin doesn't have to do this work, so by his own choice, he is able to enjoy it. His involvement in manual work allows him to forget about the things he cannot control and experience the bliss of being human and taking delight in what is accomplished. The consistent rhythm of physical labor allows Levin to forget his problems; in a similar way, the rhythm of our monastic labor allows us to lift our minds to God.

Participating in God's work by working with our hands and physically building or shaping something material is fundamentally human. Genesis 2:15 reads, "The Lord God took the man and put him in the garden of Eden to till it and keep it." After the fall, God told Adam, "By the sweat of your face shall you eat" (Gn 3:19). Work now involves hardship and labor. While it is part of what makes us human, we struggle with it because of the fall.

Sometimes it is difficult to put oneself into the work, and that is where it becomes a form of asceticism, an act of self-denial and self-gift for a holy purpose. Because all our lives involve hardships, work can be a penitential practice; we work with our hands to work out our salvation.

Jesus said, "The kingdom of heaven is like leaven that a woman took and hid in three measures of meal, till it was all leavened" (Mt 13:33). If you've ever made bread, you know it takes patience, consistent effort, and careful kneading. If you rush it, you've got dense or doughy bread which is sometimes not even edible. A sister wryly once joked, "Housewives used to be happier in their marriages because they worked out their frustrations by kneading dough. Now, they have machines that do it for them and they walk around frustrated" — which is a relevant message about the effects of the physical effort of work and patience. Sometimes we cannot take short-cuts to make our work easier because patience and effort are necessary lessons.

Every novitiate sister has had the experience of diligently taking care of some plant or tree. She gives it water, nourishes it, and cares for it only to eventually see it get sick and die. It can be disheartening to walk outside and see the first tree you planted and cared for so lovingly — now ten years old — become infected by beetles and rendered beyond help. But it's also instructive, because "we know that in everything God works for good with those who love him, who are called according to his purpose" (Rom 8:28). We *know* our efforts will inevitably fall short. We *know* that even if we try as hard as we can, we cannot produce growth — only God can.

Of course, there are many times when work *feels* meaningless and fruitless as we watch our efforts crumble before our eyes. Yet even when our plants die or our time seems wasted, at the end of the day we can still say with Saint Paul, "I planted, Apollos watered, but God gave the growth" (1 Cor 3:6).

Through work, nuns also share the common lot of the poor; even Saint Paul worked as a tentmaker so as not to be a burden on the communities in which he ministered. Ironically, one sign of religious poverty is that we are never unemployed but continually busy. We joke that there is no retirement for nuns, even if, as a sister ages, her work becomes far less laborious or more consumed with prayer. In this way, work has value as a spiritual exercise. A ninety-year-old sister can still fold towels. Our work serves the common good and builds up charity through cooperation.

Of course, all charity is one so, in a certain sense, "God gets everything," even the acts of love we have for our neighbor through good works. Good and fair distribution of work is important, because to deny a sister work is to deny her a sense of belonging, and by sharing in this labor of love, we are brought together as a community.

An added benefit of work is that it reduces the psychological strain of long prayers and refreshes the mind through the simplicity of thoughtful recollection. Most monastic tasks involve activities like cooking, cleaning, washing, sewing, gardening, and making handcrafted items — straightforward tasks that permit the mind's refreshment. The simple life of the Holy Family at Nazareth serves as a model for our work.

"Since the future of the monastery to a great extent depends upon the adequate formation of the nuns," say our Constitutions, "this must be provided for with great care, so that those who wish to follow Christ according to our manner of living may be led to the fullness of the cloistered life" (LCM 111, I). During a nun's initial formation, some of her work time is taken up with classes taught by the Novice Mistress or other sisters, on topics including:

- Prayer
- Sacred Scripture
- Theology of the Spiritual Life
- Monasticism
- Church History
- Dogmatic and Moral Theology
- Liturgy and the Sacraments
- History of Spirituality and of the Dominican Order
- The Constitutions
- Consecration and Vows

Of course, formation begins in the novitiate and continues throughout our entire lives, as we are continually conformed to Christ crucified. These classes set the initial stage and give the sisters the "milk" so that they will be ready for "solid food" (1 Cor 3:2). "The monastic community forms a school of charity whose master is Christ our Lord. In it all the nuns cooperate according to their position and function" (LCM 111, III).

This foundational point gets to the meaning behind everything we do. Following Christ, we cooperate with each other in love to build a school of charity. Most newcomers have observed that the monastery is like a well-oiled machine (or a little city in itself) where most everything we need is here, and we each do our own part to keep the machine running. United in the Body of Christ, each sister does her part according to her abilities.

And there is a lot of work to be done! The monastery needs Sister Sacristan to prepare everything for Mass or special liturgies and Sister Bursar to pay the bills. Sister Cook prepares the meals, and Sister Kitchen Helper does the dishes. Sister Music Directress trains us to our hymns and chants, Sister Maintenance keeps things running, Sister Seamstress creates and mends our habits, and Sister Librarian organizes the library. Our Sister Soapmakers create soaps and candles for our own use and to sell in the gift

shop, while Sister Shipper mails out those online orders.

All this work is done for love for the Lord and for one another. In Saint Basil's rule, he writes, "The monk is to go to his work with readiness, enthusiasm and full attention. He is to strive to work conscientiously because he knows that his true and ever-present overseer is none other than the Lord himself."[6] Our work is carefully done, never hasty, sloppy, or delayed through procrastination because we must give an honest account of our stewardship to God. The dignity and value of work comes out of the love with which it is accomplished; this is the underlying principle of our labor.

We are not overly concerned with the output of our work. "Excessive activism which would disrupt the contemplative life is to be carefully avoided" (LCM 106, IV), advises our Constitutions, and, "With confident trust in the providence of their heavenly Father, the nuns should not be overly concerned with the return from their work. Nevertheless, the prioress and those who direct the work should secure a just remuneration" (LCM 109). At the end of the workday, God is in control, and the reward and fruits of efforts undertaken are still dependent upon His Providence. We do the best we can and trust that God will take care of us.

Monastic work is not about profit but about the amount of love you put into the work you do. We read in the Rule of Saint Augustine, "In this way, no one shall perform any task for her own benefit but all your work shall be done for the common good, with greater zeal and more dispatch than if each one of you were to work for yourself alone. For charity, as it is written, 'is not self-seeking,' meaning that it places the common good before its own, not its own before the common good" (RA ch. 5, par. 31). We work together, with all the different talents and gifts of each sister in this harmonious little community, to support and sustain ourselves both physically and spiritually as we share in the work of our Creator and work out our salvation.

Martha and Mary can help us illustrate the necessary balance between prayer and work. St. Teresa of Ávila was adamant when she wrote to her nuns, "Martha and Mary work together."[7] We are completely dedicated to prayer, yes, but we must still eat and pay the bills, so our interior "Mary" and "Martha" must work together in charity.

Interestingly, when one aspect is weak, the other one is usually not doing well, either. Even though we are contemplatives, we can still act like Martha and, even though we are active, we are still called to have the heart of Mary. Each has a time and place, and while each of us might tend more naturally to be a "Mary" or a "Martha," if the two instincts are not in balance, the stress is felt by the entire community.

Prayer comes first; any nun will tell you that it is easier to do one's work after first taking the necessary time and disposition for prayer. It is a strange, amazing reality that taking time for prayer — even when one is sure there is not an extra minute in the day to allow for it — somehow helps everything get accomplished in a downright weird and inexplicable, time-bending way. Try it yourself, and you'll see! We imitate Mary at the feet of the Lord as we go about our daily tasks like Martha, but blending her work with constant dialogue and prayer. Mysteriously, powerfully, the nuns in the monastery are both contemplating and preaching without going anywhere. In the cloister, the nuns receive the Word in silence; they understand their vocation within the cloister, and the Word goes out.

A friend once marveled, "You cannot possibly do all the things you can do!" It is not possible to do everything all at once, but we are stewards of the gifts God has given us, including time. We have an obligation to complete the duties that we have been assigned for the good of the community and even just doing little things that need to be done without being asked directly. Nothing is subordinated to our life of prayer, and yet prayer paradoxically moves the work forward. How often do daily tasks (even unnecessary tasks like watching TV or movies, or scrolling social media) subordinate your prayer life?

Next, we'll look at our beloved enclosure. Why beloved? Because withdrawal from the world enables us to be free for God alone.

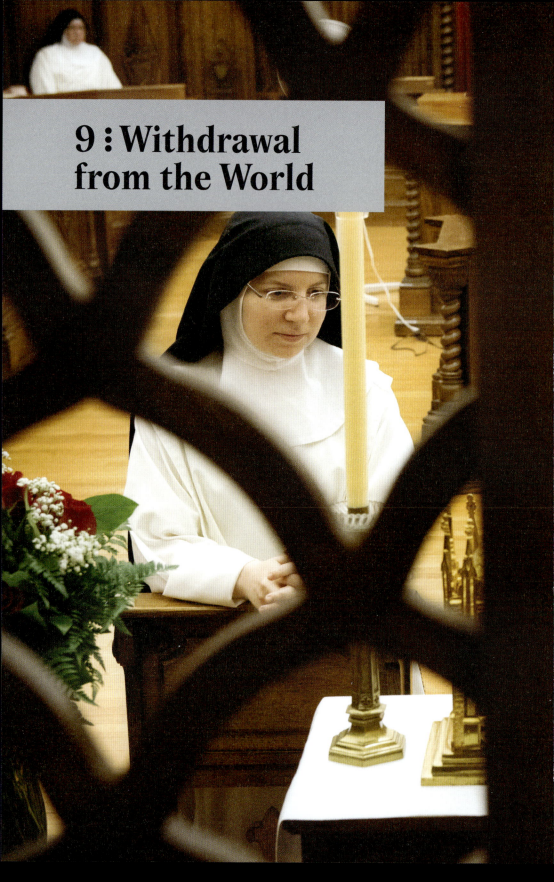

9 : Withdrawal
from the World

•••

*Your life is hidden with Christ in God.*

*— Colossians 3:3*

•••

I once had an ear infection that took the doctor half a minute to diagnose, so she used the free time to ask me questions about religious life. She wanted to know why we live "hidden away" in the monastery. I tried to explain how, since our lives are dedicated entirely to God and completely set apart for Him, our prayers are, for that reason, so much more powerful. We call our being set apart (how we stay in the monastery and normally don't go out or let other people in) "enclosure." As I was rambling on, the concept clicked for her, and she gave me an analogy of her own: "If a person spends lots of time watching trashy television, that's what they are going to be 'full' of."

Just so, and isn't that wonderfully observed? What we give ourselves over to, we tend to become, or at least to model. She struck on the truth that the psalmist asks and answers: "Who shall ascend the hill of the LORD? / And who shall stand in his holy place? / He who has clean hands and a pure heart, / who does not lift up his soul to what is false, / and who does not swear deceitfully" (Ps 24:3–4). Enclosure gifts us with the incredible blessing of being "free for God alone" (LCM 1, I). We have left the world, but in a way, we are more present in the world, more fully alive within its body. Saint Irenaeus captured this contemplative spirit when he wrote, "For the glory of God is a living man; and the life of man consists in beholding God."

Monastic enclosure has been described as a kind of power plant, its restrictions meant not to keep the nuns in, but to keep others out, so the monastery's vital workings are not impeded. Again, just so! The exterior dimensions of enclosure are the physical things: the ten- to twenty-foot walls, the material separation in the parlor, the grille in the choir, the lack of active ministry, limited visits, etc.[1] There are basic norms spelled out by the Church, specified in the Constitutions particular to each order, that we only leave the monastery for health care or other necessary business reasons with the prioress's permission. Parlor visits are limited to what is prudent, necessary, and charitable. Written correspondence, phone calls, video conferencing, email — all are used with discretion, moderation, and with specific, intentional intervals between uses. In our monastery, for instance, phone calls to family are approximately once every six weeks. Rather than being constantly connected via text messaging, we seek to be "constantly connected" to (and through) the One who loves us more than we can ever imagine. We are to be adequately informed about current events, but it is not necessary (or always good) to know all the details.

These exterior dimensions of enclosure are more obvious and radical to the outside observer, but our interior observance of enclosure is vital, no matter where we are. "By their hidden life [the nuns] proclaim prophetically that in Christ alone is true happiness to be found, here by grace and afterwards in glory" (LCM 1.V).

## Remaining with the Word

St. Gregory of Nyssa wrote, "When the Lord invites the blest to their inheritance in the kingdom of heaven, He does not include a pilgrimage to Jerusalem among their good deeds."[2] In other words, at the last judgment, Christ will not ask us if we made a great pilgrimage; rather, we will be judged based on how we've loved.[3] Love is the motivation behind our willful separation, and throughout the years our enclosure has served as an aid to growth in love.

From the beginning, enclosure was an act freely embraced by nuns themselves, and at times throughout history (during the Reformation and the French Revolution), nuns have had to fight to keep their walls and grilles because the gift of withdrawal frees us to sit at the feet of Jesus (Lk 10:38–42) and to live a hidden life of repose in Christ, devoted to contemplation.

And this stands as an eschatological sign of the Kingdom. As a community with one mind and heart, we push forward to our ultimate happiness. Our sacred space of separation is completely directed to the contemplation of the mystery of salvation revealed in Christ, a mystery of communion in Love, which we have been called to share (see Eph 3:19, Jn 3:16).

We have this blessing provided to us as cloistered nuns, but lay people can and should also carve out a "sacred space" for prayer, a place where you can be alone to encounter the Word, free from worldly distractions. For example, if you can't find a nearby church or adoration chapel, then make a designated spot in your home, or a quiet bench outside your work that you can visit during breaks, etc. To meet the Word, it's essential to have a specific place and a specific routine that includes silence, if possible.

## Purity of Heart

Enclosure is about creating a space to be filled with God. The cloistered life is essentially a battle for purity of heart. The idea of "seeing" with the heart is something that has always helped me. Generally, you think about what you see — your family, friends, loved ones, house (what needs cleaning), car (what needs fixing), favorite shopping places (when they are having sales), etc.

But in the monastery, for the most part we see the same people and the same place every day. Slowly, we start to think less about what we see with our eyes and more about what is in our heart. The banality of everyday sight causes us to go deeper. Someone we haven't seen in years can become just as present to us as a sister or as a friend we made right before we entered.[4] This ability to think with the heart is a fruit of faithfully living the enclosed life day after day, a sort of clearing the traffic or distractions of the soul. Saint Antony is said to have taught, "He who settles in the desert is rid of three wars: that of the ears, that of the tongue, and that of the eyes. Now he has only one war: the war of the heart." To give our hearts to God is a daily choice and a daily battle. Enclosure is not about leaving behind the cares of the "big, bad world" and looking for selfish, personal peace; instead — to the extent that a nun enters more deeply into God — it's about taking on the cares and concerns of her neighbors. We are still just as much "in the world," living and breathing on the same planet, but enclosure has enabled us to enter more profoundly in reality, and with a perspective of eternity. Mysteriously, our hearts become more aware of (and feel more deeply) the cares and concerns of our brothers and sisters beyond the enclosure.

## The Missionary Heart

At my solemn profession, two wonderful Dominican active sisters came to the celebration Mass and greeted me afterward. They gifted the community with a reusable cloth handbag with a wonderful picture of Saint Dominic walking along in Southern France barefoot, with his shoes over his shoulder and staff in hand. One said to me, "Even though you are a nun, you're still an itinerant preacher!" Since its foundation, the Dominican order has been characterized by its itinerancy, the moving about from place to place. How does an itinerant heart exist within an enclosed nun?

It's about being a missionary. That sounds odd, but many sisters have shared that while discerning their vocation, they felt that a specific location within the missional field was simply too "confining." By choosing enclosure we do not flee from people or problems, but — with the drive of missionaries — we become willingly occupied with the concerns of God (who transcends time and space), and thus able to enter into, and embrace more deeply, the reality of the world's people and problems.

Saint Thérèse famously explored this theme in her autobiography, *The Story of a Soul*, saying, "I saw and realized that love sets off the bounds of all vocations, that love is everything, that this same love embraces every time and every place. ... O Jesus, my love, at last I have found my calling: my call is love. Certainly, I have found my place in the Church, and you gave me that very place, my God. In the heart of the Church, my mother, I will be love."[5]

How can one spend oneself for souls? With growth, this fervent urge to save souls becomes a kind of white martyrdom, every day, every hour, every moment at the service of the Word — whether that service means the spatial limits of enclosure or the social limits of raising children. White martyrdom is a bloodless total self-offering to God. Unlike red martyrdom, it is not a one-time event, but rather a daily dying to self, the world, and its allurements. Just by

faithfully being here, we positively impact the lives of thousands.

## "Go and Preach"

People will often ask, "Don't you miss your family and friends a lot? Is it hard not talking to your family every day?"

Of course, I miss them, but in many ways, I also feel closer to them now. Because I only talk to my family for about an hour every six weeks, our conversations have become more focused and meaningful. The intensity with which I love these people has increased significantly since entering. They mean more to me than ever, and I hold them in my heart and in my prayer at all times, united and sharing in the hundredfold of blessings.

One time I was called to the parlor to meet with a Protestant minister who frequently prays in our chapel. He said, "Now! Let me ask you a question!" Instantly, begging for the Holy Spirit, I replied, "Sure ..."

Completely unaware of my hesitation, he went on, "Now the Bible says, 'Go ye and preach to every living creature ...' but you don't go out! So, how does that work?" (Mk 16:15, KJV).

With a sigh of relief, I told him about the vision of Saint Dominic: One night while praying in St. Peter's Basilica, Saints Peter and Paul appeared to him. He had been fervently seeking the intercession of these two missionaries, and now here they were commissioning him to "go and preach" saying that he, Dominic, had been called to this ministry. In an instant, they vanished, and the visionary Dominic saw his friars in pairs traveling throughout the world.

The "go" has always been the dynamic aspect of the order, and as cloistered nuns, our real work is in the choir, to which we *go* again and again, all day long, to praise God and intercede for the world while wholly dependent upon God's providence. Our participation in the holy preaching of the order is to be attentive to the Word, to be keepers of the Word, and to be doers of the Word. In this mysterious way of *going* to the choir, we "preach" the Gospel to every living creature.

The first lines of our Fundamental Constitutions read,

> The nuns of the Order of Preachers came into being when our holy
> Father Dominic gathered women converts to the Catholic faith in

the monastery of Blessed Mary of Prouille. These women, free for God alone, he associated with his "holy preaching" by their prayer and penance. Our holy Father drew up a rule to be followed and constantly showed a father's love and care for these nuns and for others established later in the same way of life. (LCM 1, I)

One of the most interesting paradoxes of our life is how we are contemplatives in an apostolic and evangelical order, how we are "free for God alone" yet share fully in its mission. Though they seem contradictory, these two dimensions are interrelated. Enclosure is important to apostolic fruitfulness. It's not simply that friars preach while nuns pray. Both are wrapped up in this twofold action, like the wheels of a bicycle turning together. Both pray and both labor for the work of the salvation of souls. There can be no effective evangelization, no preaching, without first contemplation and prayer. True, contemplation can function like a unicycle without preaching, and contemplation is not always manifest in good preaching. But prayer has a way of visibly transforming us. One cannot be a good preacher without a dedicated prayer life. Preaching needs contemplation as a source; that fullness of contemplation overflows into preaching.

Consecrated women bring the unique experience of our relationship with Christ into the holy preaching due to our particular manner of hearing, studying, and keeping the Word, the distinctive way we respond "yes" to God. This is the feminine genius of Mary's *fiat*. The attitude of a contemplative is one of receptivity and vulnerability, but it doesn't stop there. Like the empty womb of Mary before the Annunciation, we need a disposition of humble receptivity so that we too may be filled with the "fullness of God" (Eph 3:19).

As *Verbi Sponsa* points out, the contemplative nun relates to the Church as the Blessed Virgin did at Pentecost, for, "Just as in the Upper Room, Mary in her heart, with her prayerful presence, watched over the origins of the Church, so too now the Church's journey is entrusted to the loving heart and praying hands of cloistered nuns."[6] The mission of the order is the preaching of the gospel and the salvation of souls. The collaboration between those two aspects shows how the preaching is never for its own sake. It is always something that is diffusive, shared, and spread freely. This is an important aspect of preaching; it is never self-contained. There is always that dimension of it "going out."

## Extern Sisters

"Well, who does your grocery shopping?" According to our monastery directory, "The extern sister is a member of the monastic family professing the same rule and constitutions as the nuns, with certain accommodations by reason of her proper status. Her specific vocation is to serve the cloistered sisters' life of withdrawal and silence by caring for needs outside the enclosure and to offer charity and monastic hospitality to all those who come to the monastery."[7]

The vocation of an extern religious is a rare and unique calling; her role varies greatly from community to community. Devoted to the monastery's business outside the cloister, extern sisters are concerned with the temporal care of the nuns. For this reason, she is not bound to papal enclosure or the Liturgy of the Hours and is dedicated to the external needs of the monastery.[8] On a practical level, she may be assigned as guest mistress, sacristan, or portress, but she has many roles: representing the community at public events, grocery shopping, making airport pick-ups (family members or women discerning their vocations), driving a sister to the doctor or hospital. Often, she is the face of hospitality for the community.

Externs are a wonderful blessing, and nothing is lost by their not conforming to papal enclosure, as St. Philip Neri has said: "To leave our prayer when we are called to do some act of charity for our neighbor is not really a quitting of prayer, but leaving Christ for Christ, that is, depriving ourselves of spiritual sweetness in order to gain souls."[9]

## An Eschatological Sign

The world is not even aware of how much it needs its contemplatives! In the Book of Exodus, Moses obtained victory over the enemy so long as his hands were raised in prayer. If he dropped his arms, the enemy would gain, but if he kept them raised, the Israelites would succeed (see Ex 17:11). In a similar way, "The cloistered nun is like Moses on the hilltop, arms raised in prayer while the battle rages below. We may be in one sense, as he was, above the struggle, but it is our prayer, as it was his, that turns the tide of the battle."[10]

God calls us to this life, and we choose to be here, and within enclosure we get so much more than we give up. Here we "detox" from the constant noise, stimulation, distractions, and attachments of life, but that purification takes time. Sometimes the hardship of detachment needs to be endured for a greater gain. Even within our enclosure we each have retreat days, which help us disconnect from our daily concerns to further connect with God, and to appreciate better the people He has placed in our lives to love.

This "detoxing" and reconnecting is another reason why silence and retreats are so important — for everyone, no matter your state in life. Scripture is full of images of praying in solitude, encountering God. It even foreshadows the spousal bond of contemplative life and enclosure. The lover wants to be free of any hindrances to seek the Beloved: "My beloved is mine and I am his" (Song 2:16). Enclosure is all about seeking the love of God above all else.[11] Historically, the monastic tradition has held in high regard the following Scripture verses:

- Song of Songs 4:12: "A garden locked is my sister, my bride, / a garden locked, a fountain sealed."
- Isaiah 54:5: "For your Maker is your husband, / the LORD of hosts is his name; / the Holy One of Israel is your Redeemer, / the God of the whole earth he is called."

- Hosea 2:14, 19–20: "I will allure her, / and bring her into the wilderness, / and speak tenderly to her. … And I will espouse you for ever; I will espouse you in righteousness and in justice, in steadfast love, and in mercy. I will espouse you in faithfulness; and you shall know the LORD."

Of course, this applies to both men and women.[12] Spousal love is a wonderful analogy and image of the love Christ has for His Bride, the Church. A full exploration of this lies outside the scope of this work,[13] but briefly, every consecrated woman is a bride of Christ and a figure of the Church through fruitfulness and virginity; in a special way, monastic women display the spousal character because enclosure allows them to be solely dedicated to the works of the Lord and His pleasure (see 1 Cor 7:32). Whereas active religious have their apostolates, cloistered nuns are free even of this good, holy work in order to be "anxious about the affairs of the Lord, how to please the Lord."

Within enclosure, our tranquility of order and peace is established as a haven, a place where no one shall go in and no one comes out. Of course, we know that saints continue to be added to the number in heaven, and in our

community, postulants continue to join (and occasionally decide to leave), but this monastic life is marked as a prophetic sign, a foretaste of what we will experience in heaven. It stands as a reminder to "seek that which is above" while still here on earth (Col 3:1). Because Christ ascended into heaven, He leads the way for us to follow and even leaves us His abiding presence in the Eucharist. Until we join Him in heaven, we continue to carry out His mission here on earth through the Holy Spirit working in our lives.

There are practical aspects of enclosure as well. We take turns answering what we call "the turn." While this refers to a barrel-like turnstile on which items are placed to bring them into the enclosure, "the turn" mostly consists of answering the doorbells and phones, where we will confront anything from prayer requests to food donations. In this way we encounter Christ in our brothers and sisters.

We often hear of someone who came to our chapel because they saw "the church on the corner" and stopped to say a prayer. This is another sort of preaching we offer those around us: having our chapel doors open from six in the morning to seven in the evening. Each day, this place makes an invitation to everyone who passes by that God is here waiting for them. We stand as a reminder of that eschatological sign of the kingdom of God and a prophetic voice in the world.

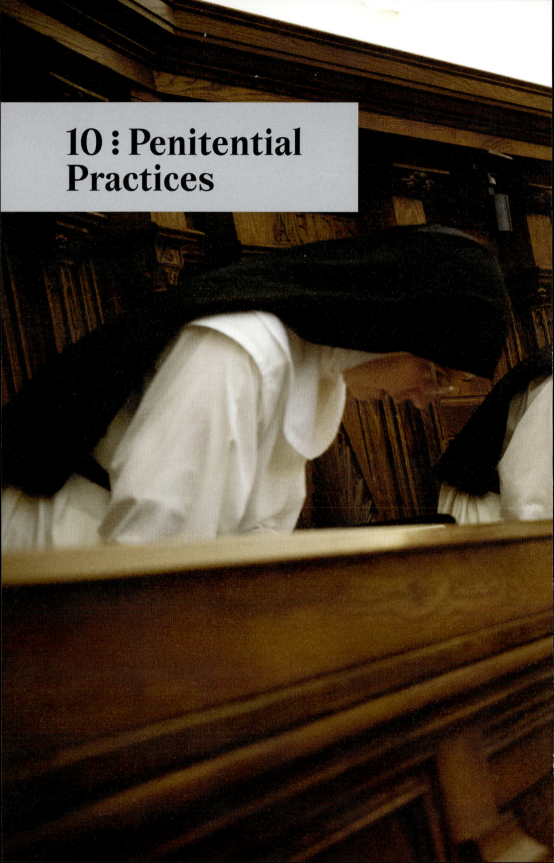

# 10 : Penitential Practices

•••

*Now I rejoice in my sufferings for your sake, and in my flesh I complete what is lacking in Christ's afflictions for the sake of his body, that is, the church.*

*— Colossians 1:24*

•••

All the aspects of our life are ascetical and present opportunities for penitential practices. An "ascetical practice" is a spiritual or bodily practice of self-discipline intended to promote growth in virtue. That may not be their *primary* purpose, but the practices are intended to serve as purifying elements to help us attain our end goal of eternal beatitude.

Once, the novitiate sisters were discussing that ultimate happiness. One sister observed, "If I know my final goal is to get to heaven, and every act I make is directed toward that end, then why do I sin so many times, repeating an act or actions that seems to not be directed toward that end?"

In a flash, the youngest postulant replied, "Because your will is weak!"

While that answer is far from complete (your passions can be driving you, not subject to reason, or your intellect can be weak or ignorant), it is insightful. For as Our Lord explicitly states, "The spirit indeed is willing, but the flesh is weak" (Mk 14:38). The truth is that our wills are weak, and it is by sometimes saying "no" to our superficial desires that we gain the strength to be and to do good — that is, to say "yes" to God more fully. The Christian tradition calls this way of self-denial "penance" or "asceticism," and it is a central part of monastic life.

This story really captures our desire to work out our salvation (Phil 2:12). The one who loves God mortifies her own self-love, because it gets in the way of love of God, and nuns are "urged more than the rest of the faithful to deny [ourselves], take up [our] cross, and bear the death of Jesus in body and soul, that [we] may merit the glory of the resurrection for [ourselves] and for others" (LCM 61, I). So like John the Baptist, "he must increase but I must decrease" (Jn 3:30). This focus on Christ's centrality inspires all our works of penance, for He is our beloved. Our attention should never be turned toward ourselves, but toward Him. In this way, mortification is not sought as an end, but as a way and means of being transformed into Christ.

It can't be said enough: *Knowing you are loved by God is necessary for loving God.* The more aware we are of God's love for us, the greater our longing to love God.

But the deliberate strengthening of our wills can only take us so far. To believe or even to think that we can accomplish any good (let alone salvation) on our own is pure folly. The entire spiritual life hinges on two principles:

"Apart from me, you can do nothing" (Jn 15:5), and "I can do all things in him who strengthens me" (Phil 4:13). These give grace its proper primacy while still emphasizing our role in responding to, and cooperating with, that grace. With infinite wisdom, God allows us to collaborate in working out our salvation, since grace perfects nature. We know "hope does not disappoint us, because God's love has been poured into our hearts through the Holy Spirit that has been given to us" (Rom 5:5). The desire and yearning for God is also the reward of our hope, so in a way the reward of this joyful expectation is God himself, who by grace makes himself known: "I live by faith in the Son of God, who loved me and gave himself for me" (Gal 2:20).

Of Saint Dominic's personal writings, we have only a short letter he wrote in 1220 to the Dominican nuns in Madrid. "Daughters," he addresses them, "fight the ancient adversary insistently with fasting, for only he will be crowned who has striven according to the rules." His point is that their battle against evil can be fought successfully only by combining it with penitential practices. "From now on," he continues, "I want silence to be kept in the forbidden places, the refectory, the dormitory, and the oratory, and your law to be observed in all other matters. ... Be not sparing of discipline and vigils. Be obedient to your prioress. Avoid talking idly to one another."[1] In short, these practices — like keeping silence — are the key without which their good intention to be holy cannot be successful.

Saint Dominic's wise exhortation requires balance when put into practice. Shortly after Dominic's death, his successor as Master of the Order — Bl. Jordan of Saxony — directed other Dominican nuns, "Do not fast too much from food and drink and sleep but be moderate and patient in all things."[2] Penance is not the goal, but an instrument to achieve it. If we lose sight of the fact that it is not the goal, it could be all too easy to do penance to an extreme, and thus to injure our health, or even worse, to become prideful about what we've accomplished. So Blessed Jordan counsels, "Fight therefore not only manfully but wisely also, because, as Solomon says, a battle should be waged with skillful prudence. And you will then fight prudently when you put the flesh under subjection not precipitately but little by little."

Implicitly, Blessed Jordan reminds us that the spiritual life requires patience. We cannot leap to the peak of the spiritual life all at once but must slowly trudge our way to the top. "It is by progressing from one to another of the spiritual virtues that, not in a single flight, but step by step, you will climb the ladder of perfection," he writes.

Besides, those practices aren't the point of our spiritual life. The goal of penance is to repent and to give God access to our hearts. "Divine love is fostered not by corporal penances but by holy desires, pious meditations, and by the leaven of that sisterly love of which each one of you loves your neighbor as yourself."[3] This call to self-mastery takes the guiding principle of prudence and should ultimately help us grow in charity. Blessed Jordan discusses the complete necessity of penances but recommends being guided by right reason applied to action.

While grace is a free gift, entering heaven can still be quite costly. Christ warns: "Enter by the narrow gate; for the gate is wide and the road is easy that leads to destruction, and those who enter by it are many. For the gate is narrow and the way is hard, that leads to life, and those who find it are few" (Mt 7:13–14). The "cost" on our part is entering the narrow gate, that is, walking the ascetic path — the challenging path that leads to life eternal.

St. Alphonsus Liguori warns, "Miserable is that religious who, being called to perfection, makes peace with his defects."[4] That admonishment is useful for all Christians. The mediocre person is miserable because, by making peace with his defects, he loses the chance to attain a spiritually fruitful life. The decisions we make today form who we will become later. By denying ourselves small pleasures now, we train ourselves toward heaven, and toward a better and more fruitful life while on Earth.

These eternal truths never fade. God remains the same yesterday, today, and forever.

## Suffering

Saint Dominic spent his life as a mendicant preacher known for his severe exterior penance, but also for his joyful acceptance of life's little trials. The latter is perhaps more useful for us today. While walking barefoot, he slipped on sharp rocks, cutting his feet and exclaiming, "Now this is penance!" Similarly, when a heretical guide aimlessly led him through brambles and thorny paths, he preached (perhaps wryly), "Let us have confidence, dearest, we

shall be victorious, for already our sins are being washed away in blood."[5]

This "washing" is a sharing in the redeeming cross. Suffering by itself has no meaning or purpose, but joined to Christ's Passion, it is a desirable gift and blessing. Speaking from experience, Viktor Frankl in his book, *Man's Search for Meaning*, echoes this: "To live is to suffer, to survive is to find meaning in the suffering."[6] We need a purpose to be able to endure the challenges that life throws at us.

Suffering, sacrifice, or self-denial always need to be undertaken in a spirit of love and unselfish generosity. Suffering makes us more receptive and transparent to grace, preparing the way for the salvation of others, bearing apostolic fruit.

Our daily trials are simply valuable, God-given opportunities to take up our cross and follow Him. The Swiss Dominican, Servais Pinckaers, says, "We can only suffer if we love and for that which we love, or for the one whom we love. Love seems to need suffering to provoke us to teach us to appreciate it, and to lift us to the level of real love, which calls us into being and to grow in mind and heart."[7] Seen in this light, suffering that might seem meaningless becomes a wonderful moment of transformation and salvific conversion.

Pope St. John Paul II explains this well in *Salvifici Doloris*: "Human sufferings, united to the redemptive suffering of Christ, constitute a special support for the powers of good, and open the way to the victory of these salvific powers." Our suffering finds meaning united to the Passion and thus has salvific power; imbued with Christ's own suffering, our sufferings become the efficacious key to our own conversion, the key to our salvation and the salvation of others.

I am reminded again to make the most of these blessings and truly to *see* them as blessings. It is so helpful to be reminded of how Our Lord said that whoever wishes to come after Him must "deny himself, take up his cross and follow me" (Mt 16:24). And we do not need to be consciously aware of bearing our sufferings specifically *as a penance* for them to actually do so. While it's good to "offer it up," it suffices to make a general intention, as in the traditional morning offering during which we offer our prayers, works, and sufferings.

## Fasting

Fasting, moderation, and abstinence are helpful not only in our physical lives but even more importantly on our pilgrimage to the kingdom of God. Jesus gives us the necessary three pillars of the Christian life so familiar from Ash Wednesday: "Whenever you give alms ... whenever you pray ... and whenever you fast" (Mt 6:2, 5, 16). Importantly, Jesus says "when" not "if"; these pillars are necessary for the Christian life. As we hunger for bodily food, our souls naturally hunger for our heavenly homeland.

We must walk in this way to detach from our own selfishness — denying ourselves and following Christ. With fasting, we strive to make our lower nature subject to the higher. "While they know that the fasting acceptable to God consists rather in conversion and humility of heart than in the rending of one's garments (cf. Joel 2:13), the nuns should nevertheless hold in high esteem the very ancient tradition of fasting" (LCM 64). Prudently carried out, fasting properly leads away from pride and self-absorption toward conversion and humility.

Augustine's rule has this pithy line in the chapter on moderation and self-denial: "For it is better to suffer a little want than to have too much" (RA ch. 3, par. 18). Consider that when a limit is continually pushed up against,

one more shove may be all that's needed to go over the line. We are cultural-
ly programmed to overindulge in food, encouraged toward a "more is better"
mindset, which is harmful. St. John of the Cross taught that whether a falcon
is held by a thread or a rope, the result is the same.[8] Could something as simple
as regular overindulgence keep us from flying further up the mountain that is
Christ?

This is not about over-scrupulosity, but about being watchful. The Constitutions even state the necessity for adaptations to times and places. Dispen-
sations and additional penances require permissions, so that prudence is always involved.

People are willing to endure all sorts of difficult fasts (even days at a time)
to lose weight or improve their metabolism, yet some will argue against the
religious practice of fasting, saying it is too extreme and threatens one's health.
The Christian pattern of fasting embraces charity and intention, and when
practiced prudently has great and prayerful effects, belying the warnings. In
*The Life of Saint Antony*, Athanasius writes, "He possessed eyes undimmed
and sound, and he saw clearly. He lost none of his teeth. … He also retained
health in his feet and hands, and generally he seemed brighter and of more
energetic strength than those who make use of baths and a variety of goods
and clothing."[9]

This is like what we read of the three young men in the Book of Daniel.
Their abstinence from food led to more vibrant health, "At the end of ten days
it was seen that they were better in appearance and fatter in flesh than all the
youths who ate the king's rich food" (Dn 1:15).

Although I am sure there are times and places where fasting is not appropriate, and even some people who should refrain (or only fast with medical
supervision), the positive experience we read about in Daniel has been my own
observation of fasting.

A priest once shared this spiritual proverb: "Stomach too full, can't hear
Jesus. Stomach too empty, can't hear Jesus." With prudent fasting, we turn
down the noisy desires of the flesh by a notch and reawaken the spirit, to better
hear Jesus. As usual, virtue resides in the middle, and the extremes are best
avoided. When you fast, use your hunger to focus more clearly on Christ. A
good place to start with fasting (presuming you are otherwise in good health)

is simply to stop snacking between meals. Despite what your survival instincts tell you, no one has ever starved to death because they skipped their afternoon snack. In addition to practicing penance, you might even find that giving up the snack means truly enjoying your next meal. That itself is a lesson in temperance, which is not just about avoiding excessive amounts of food and drink, but being able to truly enjoy and take delight in the right amount.

When you fast and your stomach is rumbling, try meditating on how hungry Jesus was during His forty days in the desert, or how thirsty while upon the Cross. Allow this hunger to become a prayerful exercise as it raises your soul to hunger for God. Aquinas used to repeat, "God came in the flesh, God suffered for us."[10] This reminder helps recall the humanity of Christ who was willing to suffer for us and the redemptive element of our own suffering. In a participatory way we are *sharers in the sufferings of Christ* by uniting ours to His ("For just as the sufferings of Christ are abundant for us, so also our consolation is abundant through Christ," 2 Cor 1:5).[11]

Both fasting and feasting days require moderation and balance to prevent the pendulum from swinging into extremes and throwing everything off balance. When I was a novice, I read an Aquinas recommendation to eat only until one is no longer hungry.[12] Until then, I had always thought the idea was to eat until one felt full! Aquinas helped me to become disciplined about eating only enough to be able to function adequately. This applies elsewhere too. Not getting enough sleep can be unhealthy, but getting too much sleep can produce lethargy. In all our spiritual practices, the body must be balanced and disciplined.

## Silence

We know from recorded history that the blessed Dominic "rarely spoke except with God in prayer, or about God, and he exhorted the brethren to do likewise." Our Constitutions expound, "Pondering this in their hearts, the nuns should make of their house, and especially of their hearts, a place of silence" (LCM 46, I). St. Catherine of Siena developed the doctrine of the inner cell, an internal "private space" where one can go to be alone and converse with the Lord — a place to give attention to the "one thing" necessary (Lk 10:42). This does not mean one is no longer able to carry out one's duties, but rather that the private times of prayer can carry over into the activities of life (certainly this is key for the laity). We know that God dwells in the soul by grace, so this little space deep within is just a room (cell) where one can go to converse with God.

Saint Dominic urged us to imitate the Blessed Virgin Mary in the silence of her contemplation, holding the mysteries of salvation in our hearts and memories, and frequently recalling them. In this way the plea of Proverbs 23:26 is fulfilled: "Give me your heart."

The benefits and wonders of silence are not easily explained. Scripture states, "The Lord has not enabled his holy ones / to recount all his marvelous works" (Sir 42:17). So much of what takes place in prayer, or in the soul, needs to be cloaked in silence; it requires humility to be silent. Closely related to humility is receptivity. Silence provides an atmosphere for prayer and opens the door to receive the Word; this openness or receptivity is key for prayer.

People seem increasingly aware of the overabundance of noise in the world and sense a need to flee from that — to seek quiet and silence. Ravenous hunger for silence is growing. Even as one seeks silence, however, the effort is immediately flooded with distractions and thoughts of self. This is a common and eternal struggle, for all of us.

Only authentic Christian prayer can offer genuine sustenance in this domain. Christian prayer is not about techniques or concentrating on ourselves, which causes us to turn inward and creates a lot of problems in the spiritual life. Our prayer is not about myth, Gnosticism, or seeking the Absolute through a technique or system, as some non-Christian religions propose. Rather, Christian prayer is always about God — it is about being led to an encounter with the Word, Christ Jesus. It is "a personal, intimate, and profound dialogue between man and God. It expresses therefore the communion of redeemed creatures with the intimate life of the Persons of the Trinity."[13]

*Vultum Dei quaerere* states, "Silence is a prerequisite to that gaze of faith which enables us to welcome God's presence."[14] Indeed, it is not an empty silence we seek to create, but a fullness. A humble receptivity to the Word takes flame in silence, which is not a negative element, or the mere absence of exterior noise, but a quieting down so that we might hear what is in the heart. God is silence, and consequently, silence is a language of prayer.

"[Silence] is the guardian of all observance and a particular aid to peace and contemplation" (LCM 46, II). This truly has been my experience. Temptations to immediately share important news with others is natural, but by delaying that (until recreation), the news only grows in value, becoming even more joyful (or poignant, as the case may be) for the delay. Practically speaking, unguarded speech leads from one conversation to another and before long the conversations get longer; too much is shared; time is wasted; everyone falls behind in duty and discipline. To call silence the guardian of all observance is accurate. "If any one makes no mistakes in what he says, he is [perfect]" (Jas 3:2).

Silence is a sort of seeking — a distinct seeking of the Lord. Silence can seem to be a bit mysterious in that way — the lack of conversations or discourse with other human beings in order to have dialogue with the invisible, often silent Lord. Yet, as we pursue the one whom our heart loves, silence becomes about creating a space for God, which can feel full or empty.

One of the purposes of silence is to foster recollection. I have always found the example of Blessed Agnes of Jesus Garland helpful and beautiful. As the account from the Office of Readings recounts,

> While Agnes was still a child, the first thing her confessor told her was to keep herself always in the presence of God. She did this very faithfully, but not without having worked at it for more than two years with indefatigable courage. "Come, come, my soul," she would say, "you must stay with your faithful Spouse for a short while." And with that she would remain very recollected for about fifteen minutes; and then after, as if cajoling and caressing her spirit: "Come, another little quarter-hour more." In this way, helped by divine grace, she gently and without violence acquired the habit of this very important exercise, and thus her heart and thoughts turned easily to God and remained with Him.[15]

In imitation of Blessed Agnes, we can foster recollection in the same way — talking to Jesus as we are walking down the hall; talking to Jesus as we are waiting in line. Instead of letting our thoughts ramble and wander, we can turn even this into a dialogue with the Lord, directing our observations, concerns, worries, joys, and cares to Him. Our thoughts can be continually occupied with what is pleasing to Him, but this of course begins with thinking about Him and speaking to Him.

Except during Mass and other specific times, our monstrance throne is open throughout the day, making the Blessed Sacrament visible for adoration by both the public and the nuns. When the doors to the throne are shut, on the nun's side they read, "*Latens Deitas*" (Hidden God).

When opened and the Blessed Sacrament is exposed, the doors read, "*Dominus Meus*" on one side and "*Deus Meus*" on the other ("My Lord and my God"). I have often reflected on how beautiful this is as I pray there — how "hidden" God is for so many in our world today, and how much I desire that others could make that same proclamation of faith that Saint Thomas made, "My Lord and my God!" (Jn 20:28). God is present and visible in the Sacrament and yet, in a mysterious way, remains hidden. Without faith, He is totally hidden, and even with faith, visible, yet still obscure.

Scripture says, "Truly, you are a God who hides yourself" (Is 45:15). This hiddenness of God is not an esoteric characteristic or attribute, but a kind of invitation; God is found in the silence for those willing to look. Those who seek will find Him. There is a bit of a paradox in all this: Our humanness wants to believe that we are in God's favor when he feels "unhidden" from us, but we also know that his hiddenness changes nothing of his love. That's the "assurance of things hoped for, and the evidence of things unseen" (Heb 11:1).

## Horarium — The Daily Way

5:20 — Rising Bell
*The Sisters may eat breakfast either before*
*Lauds, after Lauds, or after Holy Mass.*

5:55 — Matins & Lauds (Office of Readings and Morning Prayer)
Sunday: 6:10 a.m.
Followed by Lectio/Prayer/Study

7:30 — Holy Mass, Thanksgiving (10 min), Terce (mid-morning prayer)
Sunday: 8:00 a.m.
9:00 — Work
11:45 — Sext (midday prayer)
12:00 — Dinner (main meal of the day)
12:45 — Optional Recreation
1:30 — Profound Silence (time for a nap, prayer, reading, free time)
3:00 — None (mid-afternoon prayer)
3:15 — Lectio/Prayer/Study
4:00 — Work
5:20 — Rosary & Vespers (Evening Prayer)
6:00 — Supper
7:00 — Study
7:45 — Community Recreation
8:40 — Compline (Night Prayer)

*Horarium* is the Latin word meaning "of the hours," constituting the fixed times for daily activities. It is the single, most beneficial, structural aspect of religious life, safeguarding order and harmony as we work together with one mind and heart for Christ.

Toward the end of his Rule, Saint Augustine says: "And that you may see yourselves in this little book, as in a mirror, have it read to you once a week to neglect no point through forgetfulness. When you find that you are doing all that has been written, give thanks to the Lord, the Giver of every good" (RA ch. 8, par 49). What sister can honestly say that she has done everything that has been written in this little book and finds herself in it as in a mirror? Yet this practice is exactly what we have been called to do, for therein lies our sanctification.

Usually, the right course of action is simply to be doing, at any prescribed time, exactly what the rule asks. When the bell rings for Lauds, you get up and go. When the bell rings for recreation, you go. When the bell rings for prayers, you wrap up what you are doing and put your body in motion toward the choir. Because we're human, the temptation to roll over and pretend we didn't hear it, or to sneak in five more minutes of work then dash in to choir at the last minute, will arise, but where is the freedom of grace in that? Where is the self-sacrifice? One could say, "Well, I will just spend ten minutes writing this letter to a friend or reading a relaxing book or doing an edifying educational crossword puzzle before I study," but then the deeper question becomes: Is that fidelity? Sometimes ten minutes turns into twenty, and before you know it, one study period has been wasted.

This is not unique to nuns, of course. A good question for any Christian these days might be, "How much time do I waste playing on my phone? Could I spend some of that time studying or praying?"

Of course, it will occasionally happen that something legitimately comes up, causing a sister to be late to (or miss) the call to the next activity. However, it's better to say, "Never miss twice" — to pick up the next day and not let *one* miss turn into two or three. This requires the discipline and

humility to say, "I am responsible for my choices today."

There is genuine freedom and joy in following the *horarium*. You do not have to waste time planning your day or trying to decide when to do what; instead you are free to go about what you should be doing. This is one of the many paradoxes in the ways of God which we discover when we enter the monastery: liberation through voluntary restriction.

Although we nuns have the luxury of the schedule, anyone can plan time for prayer around other fixed events in life. Perhaps you say, "Oh! 9:00 a.m., time for my *lectio*!" Instead of listening to the radio while driving to work, you can call that "Rosary time." Upon waking you can immediately ask your Guardian Angel for help throughout the day.

You can also use triggers attached to times or places, like praying a Hail Mary when going up a staircase, or immediately upon receiving some good news exclaim, "Blessed be God!" I know a sister who carries the *Veni Creator* in her pocket, and throughout the day she pulls it out to pray a line, asking the Holy Spirit for guidance. These triggers can help us to remain in constant dialogue with the One we love.

To grow in charity, one needs to be made aware of those areas in which we are falling short. Recall that the Constitutions state, "The nuns are urged more than the rest of the faithful to deny themselves" (LCM 61, I). This purifying penance is for ourselves and for others as well. By dying to ourselves, we are again building up the Body of Christ, the Church, and our growth in charity is mysteriously fruitful. This is true for all Christians, who would deny themselves and take up His cross, which is a high honor and a privilege, when you think about it.

Often throughout the day, God presents His own penances of daily life, like the roof leaking, the fridge breaking down, emergency room visits, or figuring out what to do with a donation of five hundred pounds of carrots. (Yes, all of these have really happened. Sometimes in our quiet little monastery, a single day can become fodder for a country song!)

Oddly, the penances that God chooses for us are often so much better than the ones we choose for ourselves. As we work within the *horarium*, we face such challenges and come together to pool our resources to clean up the mess (or peel carrots for the freezer) and move forward. This too is a sort of preaching together through how we live, a reminder of living on a supernatural plane. We go out of our comfort zone, reach out to one another, and support each other in love.

Fidelity to our community schedule genuinely assists us every day, helping us to curb our curiosities when they become distractions, or to hesitate before we speak, or be prompter and more attentive to the duties that come with our vocation. Even how we respond to constructive criticism or fraternal correction is well-served by our attention to our *horarium*.

The point is that God provides the day, the hours, and the opportunities, and we are called to "take up our cross" and carry it through everything, with the help of a dependable form. An occasion, a prayer, a community gathering that is missed, is gone, and that becomes a loss. So in an authentic way, our *horarium* is a way of responding to grace.

# 11 : Government

•••

*Now the company of those who believed were of one heart and soul, and no one said that any of the things which he possessed was his own, but they had everything in common.*

*— Acts 4:32*

•••

I'm often asked, "What has been the most surprising or exciting about this life, after making solemn profession?" Immediately the odd answer of "Government" comes out of my mouth, usually followed by an explanation of why I enjoy it so much.

On August 15, 1217, less than one year after the official approval of the order by Pope Honorius III, Saint Dominic did something bold that many thought was foolhardy. In fact, the Archbishop of Narbonne and Simon de Montfort questioned the prudence of this decision, which was to disperse his brethren throughout the world.

The order then consisted of only sixteen friars. Two set out for Toulouse, four for Madrid, six (and a lay brother) for Paris. Saint Dominic and another brother left for Rome, while two brothers remained with the nuns in Prouilhe. Dominic did this because he did not want the "grain to rot," and also to establish the preaching mission as the heart of the government of the order.[1]

Despite the doubters, this dispersal caused the Dominicans to flourish, and it parallels our style of government in the sense of being unanimously united in our service of the Gospel, despite a diversity of locations and opinions. Recall that our vow of obedience is born of charity and leads to charity, as it is always at the service of the common good within the Church and the mission of the order. Individual responsibilities matter, but the community still operates in unity. The early brethren's harmony and obedience to God saw love fulfilling the law as the order flourished. United in love, all participate in the government of the monastery.

The purpose of government is to promote and sustain the common good. We collectively seek to find the Lord, yet still like the Ethiopian eunuch we ask, "How can I, unless someone guides me?" (Acts 8:31). This governing is our apostolic responsibility, to remain in the Word yet constantly re-examine how we are living out the Gospel together.

One way this takes place on a community level is through the governmental structure, which is divided into three branches: the prioress, the council, and the chapter. These three branches always work together as a kind of triune unit. Personal responsibility through individual participation is strongly emphasized.

## Prioress

Dominicans elect a superior for a fixed term, and the style of leadership is inevitably different from person to person.

The Prioress's role is one of service in justice and love for the whole community. She presides over the monastery as "first among equals" and has ordinary authority over the community. Her main task is threefold: to foster and protect its unity in charity, to constantly promote the contemplative life, and to diligently care for regular observance (see LCM 195). She gives permissions and exemptions. Ordinary permissions include using the phone, meeting a visitor, going to a doctor, asking to be excused from Office (the Liturgy of the Hours, in choir) for a legitimate reason, eating something in between meals, or even just getting new socks. This practice is not about over-controlling or infantilizing the community; it permits the Prioress to be constantly aware of the needs and well-being of each sister and keeps communications lines open.

Canon law states, "[Superiors] are to strive to build a community of brothers or sisters in Christ, in which God is sought and loved before all things. Therefore, they are to nourish the members regularly with the food of the word of God and are to draw them to the celebration of the sacred liturgy. They are to be an example to them in cultivating virtues and in the observance of the laws and traditions of the particular institute" (619). This is a tall order for any individual, but it is the task to which God calls superiors, because the authority in religious life is tied to an office.

We do not obey our superior because we like her and want to please her, or because we hope it will somehow benefit us; rather we obey to serve the common good. The needs of the community call for our cooperation, and the Prioress serves those needs by eliciting our consent. Sometimes she needs to charitably correct an individual sister, and other times she is called upon to play peacemaker between disparate sisters.

This role is a great burden, which makes it important to keep the Prioress in our prayers. Saint Augustine concludes his chapter on Governance and Obedience by saying, "It is by being more obedient, therefore, that you show mercy not only towards yourselves but also towards the superior whose higher rank among you exposes her all the more to greater peril" (RA ch. 7, par. 47). It logically flows that we make our Prioress's job easier through our obedience,

a continuation of "God's mercy and yours" by the submission of our will. The superior has reasons for asking what she does, and we obey as a mercy toward the community to which we have pledged ourselves, for life.

To live obedience well, it is not enough simply to have permissions or to do everything the Prioress asks, but we should actively anticipate needs and meet them — like straightening out the curtains without being asked. This notion can be applied to everyone in all walks of life. How is what I am doing at the service of the common good? How is this to the good of my family or of my neighbor? What does the person before me need, or am I simply serving myself?

## Council

Particularly in large matters beyond simple permissions, the Prioress does not act on her own but is required to put such issues before the council, sometimes to get their opinion before she acts, at other times to get their consent without which she cannot act.

The council functions under the presidency of the Prioress and, meeting at least once a month, is more involved with the economic administration and state of the monastery. The council is generally composed of the Prioress, Sub-prioress (who acts in the Prioress's stead if she is not available), Novice

Mistress, and two elected councilors. Among other things, the council approves the expenditure of larger quantities of money (more than the Prioress alone, but not as much as the chapter, and some decisions require both votes), the acceptance of an aspirant for the live-in, and admission and advancement of new members (which also involves the chapter vote).

In this way, the wisdom of the government ensures that the Prioress does not carry all the burdens of the community alone. It distributes the weight of business matters and confidentialities and operates as a sort of broad "clearing house" that works in between the two other bodies. The council can handle matters that would bog down the chapter with unnecessary hindrances. In this way, the power or authority is shared and distributed according to different capacities for the good of the whole.

## Chapter

There are two kinds of chapter: regular and conventual chapter. As regular was covered in the section on Monastic Elements, here we will cover conventual chapter — still referred to as "chapter." The monastery chapter is made up of

all the solemnly professed nuns. The community comes together to discuss our common life. Anything where the Constitutions require a decision to be made on the part of the community must be discussed by the chapter. At the discretion of the Prioress, other matters can also be brought to the chapter. The chapter is responsible for the election of a prioress and the elected councilors, and votes on admissions to postulancy, novitiate, professions, larger monetary expenditures, and all matters of major importance to be undertaken for the common good.

Key to Dominican government is that each member has a voice. Often the way the community should proceed comes from an unexpected source, just like how God uses "unexpected" saints to work great miracles. In democratic style, and with a search for unanimity, it is not a designation of the power to the majority, but a sort of probing to find the truth and go forward in charity. This sometimes involves covering the field of opinions as with a metal detector, inch by inch, beep by beep, voice by voice, until the truth begins to show itself. This conversation can sometimes be a lengthy one, but it is necessary to reliably unearth the promptings of the Holy Spirit.

Dominican Chapter is very much an exercise in listening to the Holy Spirit, who works through our sisters. Each member is treated with respect, listened to, and allowed to give her opinion. As with families, this sometimes feels like an extended hashing out of opinions, but we are seeking to live out the gospel in fidelity to our religious vocation and charism. Changing your mind, or accepting the opinions of others over your own, is a dying to self. Accepting the other is saying, "I need you" or "you have something to offer," and in this way the community becomes one mind and heart in God. In every life, such listening offers lessons for living with others and treating them with the dignity they deserve.

The chapter is the body which approves the Directory. This is the book of laws particular and distinct to our monastery, because in some cases what the Constitutions express in general terms requires specification. All Dominican nuns throughout the world share the same Constitutions, but these same laws sometimes need different applications for different monasteries. For instance, the Constitutions say, "The times and regulations for going to the parlor are to be determined in the directories" (LCM 42). Our directory specifies, "With the permission of the prioress, the sisters may visit in the parlor outside the time of Advent, Lent and the annual retreat, and preferably when the community is not in choir."[2] Another monastery may have completely different regulations.

Charity with one another brings forth a new light, shining radiance upon the encounter. Everyone deserves respect even though there may be differences of opinion. Often through dialogue, with an attitude of openness and charity, a person may begin to see the light of truth. Guided by the founding principle of the Christian life, "As you did it to one of the least of these my brethren, you did it to me" (Mt 25:40), charity transforms how we approach and relate to the world. At times, the quest for unanimity can be elusive. There are times when we leave chapter not exactly convinced, but willing to submit to what the majority in the community want, because we have heard their reasons and trust in Providence.

The same thing can happen in normal conversation with others. Someone presents an idea, and you decide that you are completely set against it. You are not against the person, but the idea. However, if you take the time to listen and understand why they believe something to be true or the right course to take, then you begin to understand how truth is working in them. "Love follows knowledge," wrote Catherine of Siena in her *Dialogue*. Once you have heard everything out (and even if you still don't agree by the end of the conversation), you still have a deeper understanding and respect for the person and can respond with charity. If we yell, or try to force our opinion on someone, then we get nowhere.

Even with this rough sharing of opinions, it is noteworthy that — unlike the Franciscans, Carmelites, and Benedictines — throughout the 800-year history of the order, Dominican unity has never been broken.[3] Despite its discomforts, the process of allowing differing opinions to surface does not lead to lasting division; instead, it brings us together and contributes to a strengthened unity.

# 12 : Recreation

•••

*Complete my joy by being of the same
mind, having the same love, being
in full accord and of one mind.*

*— Philippians 2:2*

•••

St. John Cassian once told a story about St. John the Evangelist: One day, some brothers found the Beloved Disciple relaxing with his followers and were scandalized to see the saint, the inspired author of the fourth Gospel and three Epistles, boisterously enjoying himself. Seeing their amazement, the apostle asked one of them to take his bow in hand and shoot an arrow into the air. As soon as he had done so, the Evangelist asked him to do it again. And again. Soon the man objected, saying that if he kept it up, the bow itself would eventually break. John smiled and keenly observed that souls, too, will "break" if we do not give them their proper rest.

For Dominican nuns, this proper rest is found in our periods of recreation, which serve as a kind of "soul-rejuvenator." If we spent all our time at prayer, work, or even reading books and studying, our minds would become overwhelmed under the constant strain. The same is true for our bodies. Athletes can't train for twenty-four hours. Health in mind, body, and soul requires adequate rest and refreshment, even from the most devoted workers.

But what is recreation, really? It can be difficult for busy layfolk to comprehend what nuns mean when we talk about it. Saint Thomas elaborates on Saint John's idea of "proper rest" when he says, "It is requisite for the relaxation of the mind that we make use, from time to time, of playful deeds and jokes."[1]

The virtue that Thomas is referring to here is *eutrapelia*, which is a "pleasantness" related to playfulness, wittiness, or light-hearted fun. It is the well-earned relaxation that the mind needs, the pleasure of true leisure, and the good, clean joy that warms the heart.[2] This is the virtue behind recreation done right. It need not be the only virtue present, but its wholesome joy should lift our spirits and be a sign of the goodness of living life with Jesus and each other. It is a powerful witness not only to our sisters, but to anybody who sees our life, and it is a key tool for spreading the Gospel to those who don't know Christ. As Pope Francis said, "An evangelizer must never look like someone who has just come back from a funeral!"[3]

In the *Lives of the Brethren*, there is a beautiful story about the early mirth and joy of the Dominican order. Blessed Jordan was on his way back to the convent with a fresh batch of novices, and they were praying Compline (night prayer) as they walked along. As can happen, one of the novices began to laugh, and the laughter quickly spread. One of the older friars noticed and rebuked them, telling them to stop, which only made them laugh more. At the end of Compline, Blessed Jordan confronted the professed friar, "Brother, who made you their master? What right have you to take them to task?" Then turning to the novices kindly, he said, "Laugh to your hearts' content, my dearest children, and don't stop on that man's account. You have my full leave, and it is only right that you should laugh after breaking from the devil's thraldom, and bursting the shackles in which he held you fast these many years past. Laugh on, then, and be as merry as you please, my darling sons." They were all much relieved on hearing him say so.[4] This laughing and joy is ultimately the fruit of genuine freedom in Christ.

Joy is a characteristic trait of Dominicans. Saint Dominic was called "The Joyful Friar." There is something magnetic about someone who is filled with the joy of the Holy Spirit, isn't there? "I will greatly rejoice in the LORD, / my soul shall exult in my God" (Is 61:10). The joy of being God's children extends into everything we do, and authentic joy attracts. They say that mothers used to hide their sons whenever Blessed Jordan was coming to town to preach, because they would be so moved by his preaching and joyfulness that they would instantly want to enter the order.[5]

The contemporary living out of the joy-filled Dominican charism takes many forms for us as nuns. Here in the monastery, we have two recreational periods a day: an optional half hour at midday, and community recreation for forty-five minutes in the evening. Some sisters sit together and talk, some play cards or a board game, others knit or crochet, and some make rosaries or do other handiwork. Together, we do puzzles, tell stories or jokes; we can even go outside and play games like soccer, baseball, or just take a walk. Sometimes we're all together, other times we're in small groups or just two sisters together. Whatever the arrangement, these times are always filled with the joy of community life, as we take genuine delight in one another's company. There is a certain amount of peace that is a fruit of the Holy Spirit, which resonates after an exciting game in the backyard, the performance of a funny skit, or a friendly sister-to-sister chat.

Living out the command of the Lord — to love one another as He has loved us — is obviously manifest at these periods of recreation. We come together with heart and mind to *enjoy* and be glad in each other's company,

making the kingdom of God visibly present.

St. Catherine of Siena has something related to this in her *Dialogue*, which is worth quoting in full. God the Father addresses her:

> I ask you to love me with the same love with which I love you. But for me you cannot do this, for I loved you without being loved. Whatever love you have for me you owe me, so you love me not gratuitously but out of duty, while I love you not out of duty but gratuitously. So you cannot give me the kind of love I ask of you. I have placed you in the midst of your fellows that you may do to them what you cannot do to Me, that is to say, that you may love your neighbor of free grace without expecting any return from him, and what you do to him I count as done to me.[6]

In a monastery, as in any family, God has given us each other to help us learn how to love Him. The love we have for Him is His by right (this is the virtue of religion), but in loving our neighbor, who is sometimes not kind or loving toward us, we can truly begin to love God freely.

This act of coming together for sisterly communion fits in with our common goal of continually growing closer to God together. The Constitu-

tions say that "[m]utual understanding and sisterly communion are fostered by various forms of recreation. At such gatherings the nuns should simply and cheerfully try to make themselves all things to all (cf. I Cor. 10:33)" (LCM 6, I). Of course, this is not always a steady, smooth, straight path but one that has bumps and nooks. When living closely with other people, no matter how like-minded, it's natural for tensions to occasionally arise, but trying to avoid one another doesn't work. The sister you might be mildly annoyed at may end up sitting right next to you at the next group recreation!

And so, we must learn how to get along with everyone — and not just get along, but to truly love one another, to learn to know the other and desire the highest good for her. It takes time to learn how to love others and not try to use them for our own selfish purposes. Our love must be sincere (1 Pt 1:22). In this way, recreational periods have a dynamic give-and-take, in which love comes alive. They are also an image of the whole human person (body and soul) being conformed to the Truth, who is Christ — both creative and receptive. Giving and receiving!

Usually in the evenings, recreational times involve sharing our hopes and joys, sorrows, memories, anxieties, encouragement, or blunders of the day with one another, sometimes one-on-one or with just a handful of sisters, other times with many sisters talking together in a group. It can be a time for inspiration and uplifting conversation or just coming together to build the ties of community as we unwind and enjoy leisure at the end of a day. It also serves the purpose of helping us to pray better by relaxing our minds and bodies.

Our periods of recreation, and even how we spend our Sundays, are a foretaste and reflection of the "rest" of holy leisure that we hope to enjoy in heaven. As we read in the Letter to the Hebrews, "There remains a sabbath rest for the people of God; for whoever enters God's rest also cease from his labors as God did from his" (Heb 4:9–10). This concept of rest or leisure is much broader than simply not working. It can also be a non-utilitarian way of working, like the way in which we enjoy our hobbies. Leisure is actually grounded, not in giving, but in receiving. We need to understand and properly embrace proper respite to be able to work properly as well. Further, it also connects with the Sabbath rest, a day set aside for divine worship, and in this we are free to devote ourselves to the proper worship of God, resting in God. Leisure has a much fuller meaning than just a break from work so we can go back to work; rather, by resting in God, work exists for the sake of leisure.

Of course, recreation isn't only about community, and our "proper rest" isn't only achieved in the company of others. At about the midpoint of the day, our *horarium* includes profound silence. This is a time of prayer and, yes, rest that each sister will spend on her own. It is another opportunity to take a break from our structured day, giving us freedom for any quiet undertaking: reading, study, prayer, meditation, rest, or even a quiet hobby like writing, knitting, or painting. This symmetry between leisure and activity is essential for the flow of the day and helps to maintain a mental balance, which ensures the flourishing of the whole person.

It is important, though, to see that this leisure time is not an "idle" time. Many times, when we think of rest in the world, we think of doing nothing, but idleness is not rest, and it is not good for the soul. Your soul is made for realizing its potential, for reaching out to beatitude. Idleness is standing still, stagnating. That is not to say that everything we do has to be useful; that

would be mere utilitarianism. However, everything we do should bring us into greater harmony with God, and this brings life to the soul.

In the refectory on Sunday evenings, instead of hearing the lectures or having a reader, we listen to classical music or Gregorian chant. This provides a rest for the mind and is an invitation to appreciate what is authentically beautiful. The value of this simple undertaking cannot be underestimated. Activities, hobbies, and leisure periods should be taken into consideration by the laity. It is not dependent upon skill, because skill improves with time. If you do not have one already, take up a hobby, learn to make beautiful things, or to look at beautiful things. Bring beauty into your life. Allow beauty to prepare you for contemplation and an encounter with God.

Contemplation and appreciating beauty are an important part of who we are as human beings. We are creatures with a rational soul, and that soul is the animating principle of life and the form of the body. The rational soul, wherein lies the image of God in human beings, is endowed with the two faculties of intellect and will, and creativity is one of the key signs that they are at work. A squirrel does not knit, because it has no rational nature — or opposable thumbs. A robot might be able to knit, and it might even be trained to recite prayers as it knits, but it cannot do it with heart, mind, soul, and intention.

Thus, creative work is authentically human because it requires the freedom that God has so gratuitously given us. Even as we grow in holiness, we never abandon our humanity, and the activities or leisure we partake in reflect the image of the Creator, who is working in and through us.

These times of silence or relaxed attention to others unite us with God. When considering this creative aspect of recreation, it is important to remember the Thomistic principle that "grace builds on nature." As we grow in the Christian life, our personalities and unique human characteristics are not obliterated, but purified and transformed into the likeness of Christ through the work of God's sanctifying grace in us. Few things illustrate this point as clearly as recreation, because it is in these times that we show most strongly the spontaneity and organic face of our person. Growing in the life of the Spirit is not about automated responses or prepared answers, but about flourishing as a human being according to the design that God had in mind when He made us. Our talents are to be discovered and worked out in line with His Image.

Dominicans love to emphasize this point: Growing in grace involves becoming more of who God created you to be. Recall in Genesis, "And God saw everything that he had made, and behold, it was very good" (Gn 1:31). Our personalities are made to be perfected, not suppressed, and become perfected in Christ. It is He who is ultimately perfect — all virtue finds its source in Him — so by imitating Him, we can become most fully who we were created to be, more conformed to the image of God.

This is not a lofty idea or an unrealistic goal. We are capable of doing the Father's will by living in grace according to the "image and likeness" with which we were created. God gives us all the necessary help for attaining our perfect goal, eternal life.

In the section on enclosure, we talked about the importance of what is seen with our hearts. Here, it is important to reflect on how beauty can influence that "seeing" and orient it toward Truth and Goodness. It is another facet of the same precious gem — participating in the creative act of Him whose beauty should help us to see Him more clearly. It should bring us more deeply, more fully into reality. It should raise us to contemplation.[7]

As St. John the Evangelist emphasized, we are human beings and cannot spend all our time in contemplation. We need to love each other as children of God. Recreation is the vitality of our relationships with one another. When we are working, we know that we are working for the same purpose and cause, but through communication, we are brought together in love.

This look at recreation gets to the fundamentals of what it means to be human, created in the image and likeness of God. Beauty is profoundly important because it brings us closer to God. God created all of nature to be intentionally beautiful and to lift our hearts to Him. He gives us the ability to know and love Him through our creativity, so that through the practice of this virtue, we may have a deeper sense of what is truly beautiful and grow in charity, closer to Him.

# 13 : Our Lady

•••

*Then Mary said, "Behold, I am the handmaid of the Lord; let it be to me according to your word."*

*— Luke 1:38*

•••

When I first started discerning my vocation to religious life, I was terrified — so scared that I would not even admit to myself in prayer that God might be calling me to follow Him in this way.

Obviously, God knew this fear was going to consume and hinder my ability to listen to Him, so He sent His mother to help. He gave me Mary to lead me and guide me on this route. After I made St. Louis de Montfort's Total Consecration and gave myself to Jesus through Mary, I was not the same. Not only was I no longer afraid, only three months after making the consecration, I was speaking in front of crowds of more than four hundred people telling them about the monastery I was soon going to enter. Without a doubt, I attribute the necessary grace to Our Lady and echo the question of Elizabeth at the Visitation: "Why is this granted me, that the mother of my Lord should come to me?" (Lk 1:43).

A fervent devotion to Our Lady has been present in the Order of Preachers since its beginning. One night Dominic was praying in the chapel and had a vision. He saw our Lord, and sitting on His right was His mother. She was wearing a deep blue mantle, and as he gazed at her, he saw religious men of every order in the Church standing around, but none from his own. Heartbroken, he began to cry and would not approach.

Suddenly, she made a sign with her hand for him to come closer, but he still did not dare move, until Our Lord also motioned for him. He came forward weeping as if his heart were about to break. Then Christ asked him gently why he was so sad. "I am grieving," said Saint Dominic, "because I see here members of every religious order, but of my own not one." Then Our Lord said: "And would you see your order?" To this the saint answered, trembling, "Yes, Lord, of a surety I would." Placing his hand lovingly on the Blessed Virgin's shoulder, Christ replied: "I have given over your order to my mother's care." Looking over at the Blessed Mother, Dominic saw her draw back her mantle and beneath it, he saw a huge army of his brethren. Falling prostrate, Dominic gave thanks to God and to Blessed Mary as the vision passed away. He shared his vision with his brethren the following morning after Matins, when they were assembled for Chapter, and with fiery words exhorted them to great love and reverence for the Blessed Virgin.[1] This devotion to Mary has been a living transmitted tradition of the order ever since, and the early writings (*The Lives of the Brethren*) are full of stories about devotion to Mary.

Listening and pondering the mysteries of Christ in her heart, Our Lady was the first and best contemplative preacher, and she is our mother in the order of grace. We seek to imitate her example by, among other practices, praying the Rosary, which brings us nearer to Jesus and helps us in the unfolding of our own lives as we follow Him. Devotion to Mary is not exclusive to the Order of Preachers, or even to nuns, of course. In truth, it is essential for all people.

Mary is our mother in the order of grace from the first moment that God became incarnate within her to the same self-surrender at the cross. The *Catechism* beautifully quotes *Lumen Gentium* about Mary's role in the Church: "This motherhood of Mary in the order of grace continues uninterruptedly from the consent which she loyally gave at the Annunciation and which she sustained without wavering beneath the cross, until the eternal fulfillment of all the elect. Taken up to heaven she did not lay aside this saving office but by her manifold intercession continues to bring us the gifts of eternal salvation" (969). She continues to watch over us, guide us, protect us, teach us, lead us as her beloved children. Eve is considered our mother in the order of nature, but Mary is our supernatural and very real mother in the order of grace.

## Mary Our Model

The unity of Christ and the Church is foundational for understanding the relationship of Mary to the Church. The Church is the mystical continuation of the Incarnation, and so Mary's path is the path of the Church. At the Incarnation, Mary became the mother of Christ. Her mediation is inseparably bound up in her maternal and nuptial relationship to the mystery of the Incarnation.

The *Catechism* illuminates this unity: "What the Catholic faith believes about Mary is based on what it believes about Christ, and what it teaches about Mary illumines in turn its faith in Christ" (487). Mary's relationship to the Church flows out of how she first relates to Christ the Head — from the Annunciation, her motherhood continues uninterrupted throughout time (see CCC 969), flowing out of her role as the Mother of God and the God-bringer (*Theotokos*). This motherhood encapsulates the Church, whose fecundity is recapitulated in baptized souls. Mary, as our Mother in the order of grace, by her charity brings about the birth of believers. As the New Eve, she is "the mother of all the living," which includes all its potential members.[2] Mary is the Advent of Christ, meaning that she can go before Him and introduces others to Him. Early in his pontificate, Benedict XVI beautifully referred to Mary's journey in her Visitation as "the first 'Eucharistic procession'" in history.[3]

Scripture tells us Adam's sin mysteriously ushered in sin for all humanity: "Therefore, just as sin came into the world through one man, and death came through sin, and so death spread to all because all have sinned" (Rom 5:12). This is original sin, a resounding "no" to God. We can say that all subsequent sins are connected to that first "root" sin. In a similar but opposite way, can we say that Mary's absolute receptivity to the grace of God somehow roots all subsequent receptivity to grace by other members of the Body of Christ?

In other words, if we trace down any Christian's receptivity to grace — anyone's yes to the grace of Christ — would we find some mysterious connection to the original yes of Mary? Just as Adam's sin influences all our personal sins, could we say that Mary's yes — her receptivity to Christ's grace — is also always there, rooting and influencing our own yes?

Indeed, her resonant yes echoes down through the generations as an act of obedience to counter Adam's disobedience. This is not by any means to discount the price of the redemption that Christ won for us, but to highlight Mary's mysterious role and example. The grace she had was a pure, gratuitous gift from God.

## The Rosary

Someone once asked me if I ever found it boring to recite the Rosary each time I take my place at adoration, a question which hints at a lack of understanding about the devotion. The Rosary launches us into contemplation of, and appreciation for, the depths of God's love for us, wholly outside of time or seasons. The entirety of the gospel becomes alive for us, and the in-

sights and consolations that arise from our contemplation, or the intentions of those whose names come into our awareness, render the prayer continually changed, bead by bead, prayer by prayer, within each fleeting moment.

Heraclitus observed that one can't step in the same river twice. Similarly, you can't pray the same Rosary twice. The mysteries of Christ's life stay the same, but who we are, our daily circumstances, and thus our perspectives are constantly evolving, so our insights and understandings change, too. We may pray the Mystery of the Annunciation and be moved by Mary's humility one day, her pure faith on another, or — if we are struggling with the issue ourselves — her obedience. We begin to see how our lives relate to Christ's, Mary's, and the apostles' as we immerse ourselves in each new encounter of prayer.

Often, praying the Rosary leads me to an honest examination of conscience, or inspires me to increase my spirit of sacrifice. Being devoted to Mary makes me want to follow her example and imitate her virtue, which can sometimes help me avoid venial sin.

Focusing on her virtues also inspires a deeper love of God. When I am inclined to be annoyed with another sister, I remember Mary's complete dedication to the will of God, "Let it be with me according to your word"

(Lk 1:38). Sometimes just recalling the humility of her *fiat* to something so unthinkable and monumental can help me to relax and then respond to certain situations in a more charitable way. The generosity of Mary is never delayed. For us it is so easy to be impatient and quick to anger, but Mary's virtue was always patient, generous, and prompt.

I love to reflect on how "Mary kept all these things, pondering them in her heart" (Lk 2:19) as she witnessed the unfolding mysteries of God as they played out in her own life. In a parallel way, I aspire to that same lively charity that answers to temptations or near occasions of sin with the same spirit of contemplative sacrifice. I think about the Scourging at the Pillar — all that Christ suffered for our sins, especially the sins against the flesh. Or I reflect on His Crowning with Thorns and ask for purity of mind and heart, that my intentions may be pure in everything I think and do. I recall how Saint Dominic was characterized by bearing in the inner sanctuary of his compassion a heart for sinners, and I believe that he must have gotten that trait in imitation of Our Lady.

Reflecting on the mysteries of salvation, St. Gregory of Nazianzus wrote:

> Today salvation has come to the world, to things visible and to things invisible. Christ is risen from the dead; rise with him. Christ has returned to himself; return. Christ is freed from the tomb; be freed from the bonds of sin. The gates of hades are opened, and death is destroyed, and the old Adam is put aside, and the new is fulfilled. If anyone in Christ is a new creation, be made new.[4]

This passage gives us a frame for praying the Rosary. The mysteries of the life of Jesus are replicated in our own lives. We participate in the mysteries through prayerfully meditating on the events of Christ's life, joys, sufferings, death, and resurrection, which allows us to imitate these events in our inclinations, thoughts, words, and deeds. As we meditate and listen to the descriptions of Christ's life, we can find ways to incorporate and imitate them on our own. As the *Catechism* states:

> Christ's whole life is a mystery of recapitulation. All Jesus did,

said, and suffered had for its aim restoring fallen man to his original vocation:

> When Christ became incarnate and was made man, he recapitulated in himself the long history of mankind and procured for us a 'short cut' to salvation, so that what we had lost in Adam, that is, being in the image and likeness of God, we might recover in Christ Jesus. For this reason Christ experienced all the stages of life, thereby giving communion with God to all men. (518)

In the Christian sense, we are "reliving" the mysteries of the life of Christ, repeating Mary's *fiat*. The Mysteries of the life of Christ are not finished, historically concluded events. Rather, they are a current celebration that we can participate in. They are a sharing in the fullness of God (Who is outside of time) by participation, and this is key to understanding what Saint Gregory is getting at.

The more you love, the more you suffer. With the Rosary, everything falls into perspective. Oftentimes, I am looking everywhere but in the Temple for Jesus, and I need these mysteries to help me remember.

## Mary, Our Mother Most Privileged

Of all God's creatures, Mary most perfectly shares in the eternal exchange of the Trinity. As the *Catechism* boldly proclaims, "God himself is an eternal exchange of love ... and he has destined us to share in that exchange" (221). The Blessed Mother's every action is fueled by this love that finds its origin in the Trinity. A simple analogy that can help us understand something of the Trinity is this: The Father is the Lover, the Son is the Beloved, and the Holy Spirit is the Love that unites them. That is why Mary is our model, because she is united in that communion. Not as "the Fourth Person" but as the most privileged creature, remaining a creature. We too hope to share in that communion, while remaining creatures. She alone was granted the dignity of being the mother of God, the favored daughter of the Father, the Ark of the New Covenant, and the temple of the Holy Spirit.[5]

# Conclusion

This is a good place to reflect on how Saint Augustine ends his rule: "The Lord grant that you may observe all these precepts in a spirit of charity as lovers of spiritual beauty, giving forth the good odor of Christ in the holiness of your lives; not as slaves living under the law but as women living in freedom under grace" (RA ch. 8, par. 48).

The cloistered nun's life is all about charity, growing in love of God and love of neighbor. It is about how we answer the question Christ posed to his disciples: "But who do you say that I am?" (Mt 16:15). How we answer this question changes everything, because it can affect everything we do. We have the exhortation from Lamentations, "Let us test and examine our ways, / and return to the LORD" (Lam 3:40) — a gentle prompt for the words of this book to search yourself.

St. Thomas Aquinas gives us an important lesson from the Cross, which is worth quoting in full because it captures the essence of the Christian life and what it means to be conformed to Christ, as we strive to do:

> Whoever wishes to lead a perfect life has nothing other to do than scorn what Christ scorned on the Cross and to desire what he desired. There is not in fact a single example of virtue that the Cross does not give to us. You seek an example of charity? *There is no greater love than to give up his life for his friends*, and Christ did it on the Cross. ... Are you looking for an example of patience? The most perfect patience is found on the Cross. ... Are you seeking an example of humility? Look at the Crucified One. ... An example of obedience? Begin following Him who was obedient even until death. ... An example of scorn for earthly things? Follow behind Him who is King of Kings, Lord of Lords, in whom are found all the treasures of wisdom and who nevertheless, on the Cross, appears naked, the object of mockery, spat on, beaten, crowned with thorns, given gall and vinegar to drink, and put to death.[1]

The contemplative life, the cloistered life, the monastic life, the apostolic religious life — indeed Dominican life in its entirety — entails a mystery that simply cannot be exhausted. A life of contemplation is not something esoteric, secretive, or hidden; rather, it is simply a mystery, just as Scripture says: "It is good to guard the secret of a king, but gloriously to reveal the works of God, and with fitting honor to acknowledge him" (Tb 12:7).

My intention in having written this is to proffer ideas from our life that can be applied to yours — a few little nuggets that you can take away. This book is not meant to be a dissection of the virtues or elements of the cloistered life, only a glimpse of its unity. Like a Baroque symphony, these things can be looked at individually but need to always be seen as parts of the whole.

My prayer is that some single facet of that mystery can be shared within this text to illuminate and enrich your own life. These writings simply give a sampling of my own perspective and meditations and could never be a comprehensive look into every aspect of monasticism.

There is an old adage, "How do you eat an elephant? One bite at a time." In a letter attributed to Aquinas, he says the same thing to Brother John: "That you should choose to enter by the small rivers, and not go right away into the sea, because you should move from easy things to difficult things." Start small. Each of these chapters is meant as a stepping stone, which is why Augustine talks about observing all these precepts as free women living under grace. Saint Paul advises Timothy, "Train yourself for godliness" (1 Tm 4:7). The encouragement here is for every Christian to remove any hindrance that will impede growth.

Dear Reader, my hope and prayer is that this book will offer you the incentive to see the areas where you may need work and to hear the voice of the Holy Spirit compelling you to progress in your walk with the Lord — to grow in deeper union with Him and diffuse the good odor of Christ to those around you. Regarding this work, "If it is well told and to the point, that is what I myself desired; if it is poorly done and mediocre, that was the best I could do" (2 Mc 15:38).

Thank you for picking up this book and reading it. I hope this journey has been a fruitful one for you and I assure you of my prayers. Please pray for us, too!

# Acknowledgments

I am fully confident that this work would never have come to completion without the innumerable people who prayed for me in general and for this work specifically. I cannot begin to know or even name those who have prayed and made sacrifices, but the One who is "mighty in power and sees everything" (Sir 15:18), and bestows His blessings upon you.

First, I must thank my family, Dominican Sisters, and friends for their support and encouragement. The beloved sisters with whom I live, who have been so helpful throughout these years of monastic life and have increased my understanding (insomuch as one can understand) of the ways of God and how to seek union with Him. In addition to the wonderful nuns of my community, I am also grateful to the seven lampstands of nuns scattered throughout the world, who have helped me to formulate these ideas. Several are quoted in the text, and I presumptuously believe they would rather go unnamed, though that does not mean I am without gratitude for their generosity.

I would like to thank Jeffrey Bruno and Elizabeth Scalia, who have been like two legs that have helped this project to limp, walk, run, and hopefully soar along. Thank you and may God reward your generosity. Thank you to the staff at OSV for choosing to publish this work and putting all the effort into making it happen, especially Mary Beth, Rebecca, and Elizabeth.

Thank you to those who helped me work out my ideas by offering edits and suggestions, including Donald Keeney III, Amy Knight, Jayme Dorr, Lacy Bluml, Suzanne LaTurner, Ann Virnig, Dr. Joseph Hollcraft, and Dr. Zena Hitz. Their critiques and contributions are evident in the text, and I am grateful for the enhancements of their experience.

I am so grateful to my brothers, Fr. Andrew Hofer, OP, Fr. Raymund Snyder, OP, and Fr. John Sica, OP, whose hearts are close to the Lord; their analytical eyes have shown me paths of greater clarity, both before this work and throughout it.

Lastly, I am thankful to you, dear reader, for without you, this book would not have been. I have prayed for you and will continue to pray for you, that this simple book may be the spark of that gentle nudging of the Holy Spirit, giving you a practical way to take these principles and apply them to your own life. This "nudge" has been my own experience, and I desire the same for you.

Sertillanges says in his wonderful classic, *The Intellectual Life*, "The reward of a work is to have produced it; the reward of effort is to have grown by it." May this book, through the grace of God, inspire effort.

# Appendix I:
# Stages of Formation

## Aspirancy

Aspirancy is the time of initial contact and further mutual knowledge between the candidate and the community. In our monastery, the live-in experience is a period of three to six weeks when the inquirer lives within the enclosure, getting a firsthand experience of our way of life. The candidate can assess the community while the community is able to evaluate the candidate's maturity and suitability to our way of life. If both candidate and community see evidence of a vocation, the necessary preparations for postulancy are arranged. Aspirancy lasts a minimum of one year.

## Postulancy

The postulancy begins with the entrance of a candidate into the community. During her postulancy the candidate begins to live and learn the contemplative life, through suitable catechesis, monastic observances, and personal dialogue. She participates in classes with other sisters in the novitiate to become acquainted with the basics of the Dominican charism, prayer, Sacred Scriptures, and community life. Postulancy lasts for one year. In our community she wears a blue jumper and white veil.

## Novitiate

Her novitiate begins with the postulant receiving the Dominican habit, with a white veil, and a new name, a custom seen in scripture, where those co-operating with God and given a mission are also given a new name (Saul/Paul, Abram/Abraham, Simon/Peter, etc.). The novitiate lasts for two years, and the novice continues to receive formation in areas such as Scripture, Dominican History and Spirituality, the Theology of the Spiritual Life, Monasticism, Liturgy and the Sacraments, and Consecration and Vows. At any time during these two years, she is free to leave, and the community has the freedom to ask her to leave.

## First Profession

After two years the novice requests to make profession as a nun of the Order of Preachers. This profession encompasses our whole way of life according to our Constitutions, but at this time only obedience is professed, for three years, and then renewed for three more years. The sister receives the black veil, signifying her death to the world. The scapular, the sign of the protection of the Mother of Mercy, is blessed. In this temporary profession the young professed continues her theological studies under the direction of the Novice Mistress and begins to take a more active role in the work of the monastery. Eventually, while in these first vows, the sister leaves the novitiate dorm and lives with the professed nuns, becoming more fully integrated into the life of the community.

## Solemn Profession

At Solemn Profession the Dominican nun is fully consecrated to God in the Order of Preachers until death; she is dedicated to God, following Christ and leading an evangelical life in the order so that her baptismal consecration may achieve its effect more completely. Through growth in charity, she becomes more configured to Christ, her Spouse. Every moment of her life, no matter what she is doing, is offered as a holocaust, a continual sacrifice of praise to God.

# Appendix II :
# Glossary of Terms

**Adoring Rosary** — A rich tradition of our monastery going back to Fr. Damien-Marie Saintourens, OP, and the Nuns of Mauleon (c. 1880), consisting of a community of cloistered contemplatives devoted to the Perpetual Rosary, which is preeminently centered on Christ, the Incarnate Word, and through which we enter into the mysteries of salvation.

**Choir** — The nuns' chapel, where we gather to pray and sing the praise of God.

**Cloister** — This word can have three different meanings. First, the cloistered life is a life of a nun (or monk) in the monastery ("I am entering the cloister," meaning the religious life as a nun). Second, it is a designated space within the monastery or convent separated or secluded for the religious ("That space is part of the cloister," meaning only nuns are allowed there). Third, it is a covered walkway or open passage running along the walls of buildings. ("Let us recreate on the cloister tonight," meaning, in our house, the balcony area attached to the second floor.)

**Compline** — The last of the hours in the Divine Office or the Liturgy of the Hours, commonly referred to as Night Prayer. It is concerned with the closing of the day and looks forward with hope to resting for the night and allowing our souls to rest in God (both now and eternally).

**Divine Office** — (Also known as the Liturgy of the Hours) The prayer of the People of God, which consists of hymns, psalms, readings from Scripture, and other readings from the writings of the Church Fathers and the saints. Monastic men and women are deputed by the Church for this work of divine praise, yet all the baptized are encouraged to pray the Divine Office.

**Grille** — This is the threshold of separation and the place of encounter between nuns and those living outside the monastery.

**Habit** — The Constitution says, "The habit of the nuns, which is a sign of their consecration and a witness to poverty, consists of a white tunic, a belt with a rosary attached, a white scapular and a black veil and cappa (cloak)."

**Hour of Guard** — Our monastery has a special privilege and obligation to pray the Rosary in the presence of the Blessed Sacrament, taking half-hour turns throughout the day (except during Office) called the "Hour of Guard." We also have one-hour shifts two nights of the week.

**Lauds** — Morning Prayer in the Liturgy of the Hours. The first of the two "hinges" of prayer, Lauds is pure praise raised to God Almighty for the grace and gift of a new day and includes hymns, psalms, readings, canticles, and intentions.

***Lectio Divina*** — Also known as "holy reading," this is a slow, prayerful reading of Sacred Scripture, which allows God to speak to us through His Word.

**Matins** — Office of Readings. One of the "hours" of the Divine Office.

**None** — Mid-afternoon prayer of the Divine Office. It is the Latin word for *nine*, corresponding to the traditional ninth hour of prayer (three in the afternoon) of the Jewish people. The last of the three "little hours," it consists of a hymn, the chanting of three psalms, and a short Scripture reading followed by a responsory and the closing prayer. Because of the time, it reminds us of the hour at which our Savior died for the salvation of the world and looks forward to the closing of the day.

**Novice Mistress** — The Sister responsible for the care of the postulants, novices, and temporary professed (living in the novitiate), including their religious formation, common life within the monastery, program of studies, and regular observance.

**Novitiate** — The years of probation, trial, and testing as a young woman is formed into the way of the life of the community. It can also refer to the space within the monastery where only the sisters in initial formation are allowed. They have their own dormitory, community room, chapter hall, library, etc.

**Prioress** — Presides in the monastery and has ordinary power over the nuns. She is "first among equals," the faithful servant of the monastery who seeks to foster unity of charity, constantly promote the contemplative life, and diligently care for regular observance.

**Refectory** — The place in the monastery where we eat our meals in common.

**Regular Observance** — Observance of the Rule, which encompasses all the elements of the life. To regular observance belong all the elements that constitute our Dominican life and order it through a common discipline. Outstanding among these elements are common life, the celebration of the liturgy and private prayer, the observance of the vows, and the study of sacred truth. To fulfill these faithfully, we are helped by enclosure, silence, the habit, work, and penitential practices (LCM 35, II).

**Sacristan** — The sacristan's duty is to take care of all that concerns the sacristy and things pertaining to the divine service.

**Scapular** — The white scapular is a long, rectangular piece of cloth with a hole that fits over the head; it hangs over the shoulders and covers the front and back of the tunic.

**Sext** — Mid-afternoon prayer of the Divine Office. It is the Latin word for *six*, corresponding to the traditional sixth hour of prayer (noon). This second of the three "little hours," which only take about ten minutes each to pray, invokes God's help against the temptations and struggles we encounter at the heat (or mid-point) of the day.

**Temporary Profession** — See First Profession.

**Terce** — Mid-morning prayer of the Divine Office. It is the Latin word for *three*, corresponding to the traditional third hour of prayer (nine in the morning). The first of the "little hours," it contains references to the Holy Spirit descending upon the apostles, so in the same way we ask the Holy Spirit to bless and inspire the activities of the day.

**Vespers** — This is Evening Prayer from the Liturgy of the Hours, one of the two hinges (the other being Morning Prayer, or Lauds) on which to hang the day. It includes many references to the closing of the day and thus is ideally celebrated at sunset.

**Vestition** — The ceremony at which a novice receives the habit.

# Photo Captions

Pages 8–9: Street view of the Monastery of Our Lady of the Rosary

Page 14: The family of a Summit nun views her profession from the public chapel

Page 15: Nuns' choir at the Monastery of Our Lady of the Rosary

Page 17: Sister Mary Magdalene at prayer in choir

Page 18–19: Nuns praying the Office in Choir

Page 23: Entrance to the choir from inside the enclosure

Page 28: Inside a sister's cell (Monastery of Our Lady of the Rosary)

Pages 30–31: Changing the veil from white to black at First Profession

Page 34: Nuns praying in chapter (Monastery of Our Lady of the Rosary)

Page 37: A simple meal in the monastery (in the guest's dining room)

Pages 38–39: Prioress gives the sign of peace to a newly professed sister in the public chapel after her vows

Page 43: Sisters sharing a musical moment at recreation

Page 47: A novice prays in the nuns' choir

Page 51: Sisters doing dishes together

Page 54: Saying grace before a meal in the refectory

Page 57: An overhead photo of a sister in her choir stall

Page 58: Sisters gather as a community to select patron saints for the year

(Monastery of Our Lady of the Rosary)

Page 64: Sisters praying in choir

Page 67: At Mass, the priest faces the nuns, who are behind the grille

Page 69: A nun venerating the heart of St. John Vianney, seen through the grille

Page 73: Nuns at prayer in choir

Page 79: Dominican nuns praying in the "cruciform" posture (Monastery of Our Lady of the Rosary)

Page 82: A sister in her stall at choir

Page 86: Sisters celebrating a profession

Page 95: A sister walks in a portion of the garden at Our Lady of the Rosary monastery

Page 97: A chantress intones during the Liturgy of the Hours

Page 104: A sister professing into the hands of her prioress while her family looks on

Page 107: A sister receives a gold ring after making her final vows

Page 110: Sisters reverencing the relics of St. John Vianney in the nuns' choir

Page 115: After her solemn profession, a sister signs the profession book

Pages 122–123: The prayerful and personal work of contemplation

Page 129: Sister Organist in the choir

Page 132: A sister prays during the Liturgy of the Eucharist

Page 135: A sister receives Communion during Mass

Page 147: Study is a lifelong part of the life of a Dominican nun (Monastery of Our Lady of the Rosary)

Page 149: A nun prostrates herself before the Prioress, asking "God's mercy and yours"

Page 152: A sister at prayer in choir

Pages 154–155: A sister goes about her work in the monastery garden

Page 158: Sister Woodworker creates a pen for the monastery's gift shop

Page 161: A sister busily at work sewing

Page 163: Sister Soapmaker makes soap for the community to use and to sell

Page 164: A sister makes rosaries at recreation

Page 167: A sister going about her housework

Pages 168–169: Sisters at prayer behind the grille

Page 173: A sister in prayer before the Blessed Sacrament

Page 175: A sister intercedes for the intentions of others

Page 176: The nuns are privileged to practice Perpetual Adoration, at which their prayers embrace the world

Page 178: A sister walks through the monastery's grounds

Page 180: The community enjoys a visitor's remarks

Page 181: A sister displays the fruits of the monastery's garden (Monastery of Our Lady of the Rosary)

Page 182: The sisters are buried in their own cemetery in the enclosure (Monastery of Our Lady of the Rosary)

Pages 184–185: The nuns make a profound bow during the Liturgy of the Hours

Page 190: A nun prostrates herself during solemn profession

Page 198: Praying the *De Profundis* for the deceased benefactors of the monastery and members of the Order before a meal

Page 202-203: A sister professing into the hands of her prioress while her family looks on

Page 207: The prioress pins a nun's veil during a profession ceremony

Page 208: In the public chapel, a nun prostrates before the prioress during her solemn profession ceremony

Page 212: Two sisters plan what they want to play for evening recreation

Page 217: A sister takes a moment with Siena, the monastery's dog

Page 218: Siena, stealing a ball from a game of "monastic baseball"

Page 220: A sister embroiders during community recreation

Pages 224–225: A sister prays before a statue of Mary, the Child Jesus, and Saint Dominic

Page 230: Praying the Rosary is an important part of daily life at the Dominican Monastery of Our Lady of the Rosary

Page 232: A sister makes rosaries by hand

Pages 234–235: A sister smiles joyfully

# Notes

## Introduction

1. *Liber Constitutionum Monialium*, V (hereafter cited in text as LCM).

2. Francis, *Vultum Dei quaerere*, Vatican.va, par. 6.

3. *Catechism of the Catholic Church*, par. 1846 (hereafter cited in text as CCC).

## Chapter 1: Monastic Elements

1. Willa Cather, *Later Novels: Shadows on the Rock* (Literary Classics of the United States, Inc., 1990), 562–563.

2. *The Rule of Saint Augustine*, ch. 1, par. 3 (hereafter cited in text as RA).

3. "Institutes which are entirely ordered to contemplation always hold a distinguished place in the mystical Body of Christ: for they offer an extraordinary sacrifice of praise to God, illumine the people of God with the richest fruits of holiness, move it by their example, and extend it with hidden apostolic fruitfulness. For this reason, members of these institutes cannot be summoned to furnish assistance in the various pastoral ministries however much the need of the active apostolate urges it." Code of Canon Law, 674.

4. A tonsure could be briefly described as a "religious haircut" especially for Roman Catholic and Eastern Orthodox as a sign of consecration to God. The middle circle of hair is clipped away, leaving a crown. Cecilia Cesarini, OSB, "The Legend of Saint Dominic," ch. 14, in *Lives of the Brethren of the Order of Preachers*, 1206–1259, trans. Placid Conway, OP (Blackfriars Publications, 1955). Also in *Relation of Sister Cecilia*, n. 14. Lacordaire, *Vie de Saint Dominique,* 7th ed.,192.

5. https://www.monialesop.org/

6. *Institutes of Sisters of San Sisto and Statutes of the Sisters of Saint Mary Magdalene*, trans. Sister Mary Martin Jacobs, OP (Dominican Nuns of Summit, NJ, 2004), ch. 8, 1 "Clothing."

7. Canon 573.1: "The life consecrated through the profession of the evangelical counsels is a stable form of living by which the faithful, following Christ more closely under the action of the Holy Spirit, are totally dedicated to God who is loved most of all, so that, having been dedicated by a new and special title to His honor, to the building up of the Church, and to the salvation of the world, they strive for the perfection of charity in the service of the kingdom of God and, having been made an outstanding sign in the Church, foretell the heavenly glory."

8. Jordan of Saxony, "The Libellus of Jordan of Saxony," par. 57, in *Saint Dominic: Biographical Documents*, ed. Francis C. Lehner, OP (1964).

9. *Institutes of Sisters of San Sisto and Statutes of the Sisters of Saint Mary Magdalene*, ch. 2, 1 "Meals."

10. *Fundamental Constitutions of the Order,* IV.

## Chapter 2: Common Life

1. *The Rule of St. Benedict*, 4:47.

2. Dorotheus of Gaza, Discourse 6 §78, in *Dorotheus of Gaza: Discourses and Sayings*, trans. Eric P. Wheeler, vol. 33, Cistercian Studies Series (Cistercian Publications, 1977), 139.

3. Thomas Aquinas, *Summa Theologiae,* II-II, q.30, a.1.

4. Thérèse of Lisieux, *Story of a Soul: The Autobiography of St. Thérèse of Lisieux,* 3rd ed., trans. John Clarke, OCD (ICS Publications, 1976), 250.

5. Graham Greene, *The Power and the Glory* (Penguin Books, 1971), 131.

6. See St. Thérèse of Lisieux, *Story of a Soul*, 222.

7. William Shakespeare, *The Merchant of Venice*, Act IV, Scene 1.

8. Gabrielle Bossis, *HE and I*, trans. Evelyn M. Brown (Éditions Paulines, 1969), 189.

9. Thérèse of Lisieux, *Story of a Soul*, 222.

10. Fr. Marie-Michel Philipon, OP, *The Dominican Soul*.

11. Victor Hugo, *Les Misérables*, trans. Charles E. Wilbour (Random House, Inc. 1992), 145.

12. *Rule of Saint Benedict* 4, 74.

13. Sigrid Undset, *Kristin Lavransdatter, III: The Cross* (Random House, Inc., 1987), 401.

14. Aquinas, *ST,* I-II, q.77, a.4.

15. Augustine, *The Confessions*, trans. Maria Boulding, OSB (Augustine Heritage Institute, 1997), Book X, 29, 40.

16. Dante Alighieri, *The Divine Comedy: The Purgatorio*, trans. John Ciardi (Norton & Company, 1970), Canto III, Lines 121–123.

## Chapter 3: Liturgical Prayer

1. *Sacrosanctum Concilium,* Vatican.va, par. 7, 10.

2. Congregation for Institutes of Consecrated Life and for Societies of Apostolic Life, *Verbi Sponsa*, Vatican.va, par. 6.

3. Aquinas, ST, III, q.73, a.1 and q.79, a.7.

4. Thomas Aquinas, *O Sacrum Convivium*.

5. Victor Hugo, *Les Misérables*, trans. Charles E. Wilbour (Random House, Inc., 1992), 25.

6. Bernard of Clairvaux, *The Twelve Degrees of Humility and of Pride*, I, ch. 3.

7. See Aquinas, ST, II-II, q.83, a.13.

## Chapter 4: Dominican Prayer

1. Jordan of Saxony, "The Libellus of Jordan of Saxony," par. 7, in *Saint Dominic: Biographical Documents*, ed. Francis C. Lehner, OP (1964).

2. St. Bernard of Clairvaux, *On Loving God*, Book III, 7.

3. "Nine Ways of Prayer of St. Dominic," in *Selections from Early Dominicans: Selected Writings*, trans. Simon Tugwell, OP (Missionary Society of St. Paul the Apostle in the State of New York, 1982, Roma, 1996), 3–21. Scripture cited in this section taken directly from "Nine Ways of Prayer."

4. Cassian, *Conferences*, Book IX, ch. II.

5. John Bunyan, *The Pilgrim's Progress: From This World to That Which is to Come* (Legacy Press, Inc., 1967), 12.

6. Benedict XVI, *Deus Caritas Est*, Vatican.va, par. 1.

7. See Aquinas, ST, I-II, q.113, a.9, ad.2.

8. "For faith presupposes natural knowledge, even as grace presupposes nature, and perfection supposes something that can be perfected." Aquinas, ST, I, q.2, a.2, ad.1.

9. Francis Spirago, *The Catechism Explained* (Eighth Edition), (Patristic Publishing, 2019), 505.

10. Francis, *Evangelii Gaudium*, Vatican.va, 152.

11. Thomas Aquinas, *Sur le Credo*, nos. 895–896, emphasis added.

12. Francis, *Vultum Dei quaerere*, par. 21.

13. Gerald Vann, OP, *To Heaven with Diana* (Henry Regnery Co., 1965), Letter 31, p. 112.

14. Mother Mary Francis, PCC, *My Beloved Is Mine and I Am His: Conferences on Brideship for Women Religious* (Cluny Media, LLC, 2022), 10.

15. Fr. Herbert McCabe, OP, *God, Christ and Us* (Continuum, 2005).

16. Profession booklet.

17. The Sacred Congregation for Religious and Secular Institutes, *Venite Seorsum*, III.

18. *Lumen Gentium*, par. 10 (see CCC 1141).

19. Fulton J. Sheen, *Peace of Soul: Timeless Wisdom on Finding Serenity and Joy by the Century's Most Acclaimed Catholic Bishop* (Liguori Publications, 1996).

20. St. Gregory the Great, *Dialogues* I, 8, quoted in Aquinas, ST, II-II, q.83. a.2.

21. Francis, *Vultum Dei quaerere*, par. 17.

22. Francis, *Vultum Dei quaerere*, par. 5 (see 2 Cor 1:20; Eph 5:19–20).

23. Congregation for Institutes of Consecrated Life and for Societies of Apostolic Life, *Verbi Sponsa*, Vatican.va, par. 6.

24. Aquinas, ST, I, q.20, a.1, ad.3. See also CCC 1766.

25. Augustine of Hippo, Epistle 130, 18.

26. Augustine of Hippo, *Expositions on the Psalms*.

## Chapter 5: Evangelical Counsels

1. Also, Thomas Aquinas says, "Therefore, all the counsels, which invite us to perfection, aim at this, that man's mind be turned away from affection to temporal objects, so that his mind may tend more freely to God, by contemplating him, loving him, and fulfilling his will." *Treatise of Perfection*, ch. 6.

2. Aquinas, ST, II-II, q.88, a.1.

3. See John Paul II, *Vita Consecrata*, Vatican.va, par. 18.

4. Aquinas, ST, I-II, q.108, a.4, sed contra.

5. John Paul II, *Vita Consecrata*, par. 21.

6. Augustine of Hippo, *De Bono Coniugali*, 24, 32; *Expositions on the Psalms*, 71, s. 2, 6.

7. See Aquinas, ST, I-II, q.107, a.4, taken from Augustine's Commentary on 1 John 5:3.

8. See Paul VI, *Evangelica Testificatio*, Vatican.va, par. 27.

9. Irenaeus of Lyon, *Adversus haereses* III, ch. 22, par. 4. Also quoted in LCM 19, I.

10. Summit Choirbook (Dominican Nuns of Summit, 1971), #148. *Summi Parentis Filio*, from *Catholicum Hymnologium Germanicum* (1587), trans. Edward Caswall.

11. Aquinas, ST, II-II, q.180, a.2, ad.2.

12. Fulton J. Sheen, *The World's First Love* (Garden City Books, 1953), 31.

13. Benedict XVI and Robert Cardinal Sarah, *From the Depths of Our Hearts: Priesthood, Celibacy, and the Crisis of the Catholic Church*, trans. Michael J. Miller (Ignatius Press, 2020), 70–71.

14. Cyprian of Carthage, *On Virgins,* 22.

15. Thomas Aquinas, *Treatise of Perfection*, ch. 7.

16. Francis, *Vultum Dei quaerere*, par. 25.

## Chapter 6: Hearing and Keeping the Word of God

1. Prologue of the *Primitive Constitutions of the Order of Friars Preachers*.

2. John Paul II, *Vita Consecrata*, par. 59.

3. Congregation for Institutes of Consecrated Life and for Societies of Apostolic Life, *Verbi Sponsa*, Vatican.va, par. 6.

4. Prologue to *The Rule of St. Benedict,*     1.

5. Aquinas, ST, I, q.75, a.5; 3a, q.5.

6. John of the Cross, *Dark Night of the Soul*, ch. XXI, par. 8.

7. William Shakespeare, *Hamlet*, Act I, Scene V, in Arden Shakespeare, 2nd ed, ed. Harold Jenkins (Thompson Learning, 1982).

8. Athanasius, Letter to Marcellinus, 109.

9. See Augustine of Hippo, *Expositions on the Psalms*, 60:1–2, 61:4, 85:1, 5.

10. Antiphon 1, Office of Readings, Tuesday, Week II.

11. Aquinas, ST, II-II, q.27, a.7.

12. Parts specific to the nuns from *The Order of Reception and Profession of the Fraternal Sodalities of Clerics and Laity of Saint Dominic*. Approved by the Congregation for Divine Worship and the Discipline of the Sacraments, March 25, 1998.

13. John Paul II, *Vita Consecrata*, par. 34.

14. Francis, *Vultum Dei quaerere*, par. 10.

15. Congregation for Institutes of Consecrated Life and for Societies of Apostolic Life, *Verbi Sponsa*, par. 6.

16. St. Augustine of Hippo, *City of God*, XV.23.

# Chapter 7: Study

1. Jacques Maritain, *The Angelic Doctor: The Life and Thought of Saint Thomas Aquinas*. This famous story comes to us from a friend and scribe of Saint Thomas, Reginald of Piperno.

2. St. Catherine of Siena, *Treatise on Divine Providence* (Cap 167, *Gratiarum actio ad Trinitatem*), used in the Roman Office of Readings for the liturgical memorial of St. Catherine of Siena on April 29.

3. Jordan of Saxony, "The Libellus of Jordan of Saxony," par. 6–7, in *Saint Dominic: Biographical Documents*, ed. Francis C. Lehner, OP (1964).

4. Aquinas, ST, II-II, q.188, a.6.

5. Aquinas, ST, q.180, a.1, ad.1. *Simplex intuitus.*

6. John Paul II, *Fides et Ratio*, Vatican.va.

7. Aquinas, ST, II-II, q.180, a.4, "*contemplatio est finis totius humanae vitae.*"

8. *Rule of Saint Benedict*, ch. 4, 50.

9. I owe all the credit of this wonderful idea to Fr. Terrance G. Kardong, OSB, of fond memory. In November 2012 we were reading in the Refectory his book *Conversation with Saint Benedict: The Rule in Today's World* (Liturgical Press, 2012). On the second to last page of this book, he mentions that one of the tactics he uses to remember what he has read is to write down the titles and a brief summary. When I heard this, I thought, "Brilliant!" and immediately began doing a similar practice. He mentions in the book that it is not about trying to fly through as many books as possible or creating long lists for bragging rights; rather, it is an exercise in fixing the main points of a book in one's memory.

10. Ferrer Cassidy, OP, "Dominic's Death," *Dominicana* 6, no. 1 (1921): 6, https://www.dominicanajournal.org/wp-content/files/old-journal-archive/vol6/no1/dominicanav6n1stdominicsdeath.pdf.

11. St. Jerome, "Letter to Rusticus" (Letter 125), par. 11.

12. A. G. Sertillanges, *The Intellectual Life: Its Spirit, Conditions, Methods* (The Catholic University of America Press, 1998), 124.

13. John Paul II, *Veritatis Splendor*, Vatican.va, par. 39.

14. See Aquinas, ST, II-II, q.166, a.2, and q.167, a.1.

15. See Augustine of Hippo, *De Doctrina Christiana* II, ch. 41, par. 62; "Epistle 55," ch. 21, par. 39; and *Confessions* VII, ch. 20, par. 26.

16. See Thomas á Kempis, *The Imitation of Christ,* ch. 80 "Warning against Vanity and Worldly Learning."

## Chapter 8: Work

1. Aquinas, ST, III, q.79, a.1, ad.2.

2. Boniface Ramsey, *Beginning to Read the Fathers* (Paulist Press, 1985), 170–171.

3. "Institutes which are entirely ordered to contemplation always hold a distinguished place in the mystical Body of Christ: for they offer an extraordinary sacrifice of praise to God, illumine the people of God with the richest fruits of holiness, move it by their example, and extend it with hidden apostolic fruitfulness. For this reason, members of these institutes cannot be summoned to furnish assistance in the various pastoral ministries however much the need of the active apostolate urges it." Canon 674.

4. See John Paul II, "Address to the Religious in Burundi," from *L'Osservatore Romano* 17, September 1990, 14.

5. Leo Tolstoy, *Anna Karenina*, trans. Louise and Aylmer Maude (Dover Publications, Inc., 2004), 228.

6. Basil, *The Long Rules 41; Ascetical Works and Treatises*, trans. Monica Wagner (The Catholic University of America Press, 1962), 314–316.

7. Teresa of Ávila, *Way of Perfection*, ch. 31, sec. 4 .

## Chapter 9: Withdrawal from the World

1. It lies outside the scope of this work to give the history of enclosure — I recommend Jean Prou, OSB, *Walled About with God: The History and Spirituality of Enclosure for Cloistered Nuns*, trans. David Hayes, OSB (Gracewing, 2005).

2. Gregory of Nyssa, *On Pilgrimages*, trans. William Moore and Henry Austin Wilson, in *Nicene and Post-Nicene Fathers*, Second Series, vol. 5, eds. Philip Schaff and Henry Wace (Christian Literature Publishing Co., 1893), revised and edited for New Advent by Kevin Knight, http://www.newadvent.org/fathers/2913.htm.

3. See CCC 1022.

4. A few distinctions: I am not saying this is a perfect or better substitute. Nor am I saying that people outside the monastery are shallow and fickle while people in the monastery are heavy, deep, real, holy saints. Only that there is a mysterious hundredfold return. Also, we do occasionally meet new people (probably just less frequently than you do), but with enclosure we lose the "stimulation" of constantly changing environments and meeting new people every day. As our Constitutions state, "By withdrawal from the world, in fact and in spirit, the nuns, like prudent virgins waiting for their Lord, are freed from worldly affairs so that they may have leisure to devote themselves wholeheartedly to the kingdom of God"

(LCM 36).

    5. Thérèse of Lisieux, *Story of a Soul: The Autobiography of St. Thérèse of Lisieux,* 3rd ed., trans. John Clarke, OCD (ICS Publications, 1976), 227–229. Also found in the Office of Readings for the memorial of St. Thérèse on October 1.

    6. Congregation for Institutes of Consecrated Life and for Societies of Apostolic Life, *Verbi Sponsa*, Vatican.va, par. 4.

    7. Our Lady of the Rosary Monastery, Summit, NJ, 2018 Directory in reference to LCM 172, I–II. See also 1961 Instruction from the Congregation of Religious, "Extern Sisters of Monasteries of Nuns" and Paul VI, *Perfectae Caritatis*, Vatican.va, par. 15–16.

    8. "Some extern sisters may be included in the monastic family as determined in the directories, taking into account the prescriptions of common law." LCM 172, II and *Cor Orans,* par. 193.

    9. The Oratory at Oxford, *The Maxims and Sayings of St. Philip Neri*, 22.

    10. "A contemplative monastery is a gift also for the local Church to which it belongs. Representing the prayerful face of the Church, a monastery makes the Church's presence more complete and meaningful in the local community. (49) A monastic community may be compared to Moses who, in prayer, determined the fate of Israel's battles (cf. Ex 17:11), or to the guard who keeps the night watch awaiting the dawn (cf. Is 21:6)." Congregation for Institutes of Consecrated Life and for Societies of Apostolic Life, *Verbi Sponsa*, par. 8. See also: "In the Book of Exodus, we read that Moses decided the fate of his people by prayer; he ensured victory over the enemy as long as he kept his arms raised to ask for the Lord's help (cf. 17:11). It strikes me that this is a most eloquent image of the power and efficacy of your own prayer on behalf of all humanity and the Church, especially of the vulnerable and those in need. Now, as then, we can conclude that the fate of humanity is decided by the prayerful hearts and uplifted hands of contemplative women." Francis, *Vultum Dei quaerere*, par. 17.

    11. "Prefer nothing to the love of Christ." *The Rule of St. Benedict*, trans. Justin Mc-Cann, OSB (Sheed and Ward, 1976), 4:21.

    12. "All human beings — both women and men — are called through the Church, to be the 'Bride' of Christ." Pope St. John Paul II, *Mulieris dignitatem*, par. 25.

    13. See Thomas Aquinas, *Sentences,* IV, d.38, q.1, a.5 for more information about the link between fruitfulness and virginity.

# Chapter 10: Penitential Practices

    1. Dominic, Letter I, in *Saint Dominic*: *Biographical Documents*, ed. Francis C. Lehner, OP (1964), http://www.domcentral.org/trad/domdocs/0002.htm.

    2. Jordan of Saxony, "Letter 13," June–July, 1225.

    3. Jordan of Saxony, "Letter 10," January–February, 1225.

    4. Alphonsus Liguori, *The Religious State* (Eugene Grimm edition, 1835–1891), 85.

    5. Process of canonization, Bologna, 27. Bis. Frachet, II, 2.

    6. Viktor E. Frankl, *Man's Search for Meaning* (Beacon Press, 2006), x.

    7. Servais Pinckaers, OP, *Passions and Virtues*, trans. Benedict Guevin, OSB (The Cath-

olic University of America Press, 2017), 57.

8. "For it comes to the same thing whether a bird be held by a slender cord or by a stout one. ... It is true that the slender one is the easier to break; still, easy though it be, the bird will not fly away if the cord be not broken. And thus the soul that has attachment to anything, however much virtue it possess, will not attain to the liberty of Divine union." *St. John of the Cross, Ascent of Mount Carmel*, trans. Allison Peers,     1.XI .4).

9. Athanasius, *The Life of Antony and the Letter to Marcellinus* (Paulist Press, 1980), 98.

10. Jean-Pierre Torrell, OP, *St. Thomas Aquinas, Volume 1: The Person and His Work*, trans. Robert Royal (The Catholic University of America Press, 1996), 284.

11. For further information, see John Paul II, *Salvifici Doloris*, Vatican.va, par. 17–20.

12. Aquinas, ST, II-II, q.147.

13. "[Christian prayer] flees from impersonal techniques or from concentrating on oneself, which can create a kind of rut, imprisoning the person praying in a spiritual privatism which is incapable of a free openness to the transcendental God." Congregation for the Doctrine of the Faith, "Letter to the Bishops of the Catholic Church on Some Aspects of Christian Meditation," I.3.

14. Francis, *Vultum Dei quaerere*, par. 33.

15. "The Admirable Life of Sister Agnes of Jesus, O.P.," written by a Benedictine monk.

## Chapter 11: Government

1. Dominic was reported to have said something like, "Let me do what I will; I know what I desire. Hoarded, the grain rots; cast to the wind, it brings forth fruit." *Processus* (Bologna), no. 26; Jordan, nos. 47, 62; Ferrand, no. 31.

2. Our Lady of the Rosary Monastery, Summit, NJ, 2018 Directory.

3. William A. Hinnebusch, *The History of the Dominican Order: Origins and Growth to 1500* (Alba House, 1966), 77.

## Chapter 12: Recreation

1. Aquinas, ST, II-II, q.168, a.2.

2. See Aquinas, ST, II-II, q.168.

3. Francis, *Evangelii Gaudium*, Vatican.va, 10.

4. Placid Conway, OP, trans., *Lives of the Brethren of the Order of Preachers*, 1206–1259 (Blackfriars Publications, 1955), ch. 31, "His Prudent and Witty Replies."

5. Jordan of Saxony, "The Libellus of Jordan of Saxony," par. 57.

6. St. Catherine of Siena, *The Dialogue*, 64.

7. "The first and foremost duty of all religious is to be the contemplation of divine things and assiduous union with God in prayer." Canon 663.1.

## Chapter 13: Our Lady

1. Placid Conway, OP, trans., *Lives of the Brethren of the Order of Preachers, 1206–1259* (Blackfriars Publications, 1955), ch. 7: "How the Blessed Virgin Appeared to Him While at

Prayer, and Showed Him the Care She Takes of the Order."

2. See Aquinas, ST, III, q.8, a.3.

3. Benedict XVI, "Address of His Holiness Benedict XVI During the Prayer Meeting in the Vatican Gardens for the Conclusion of the Marian Month of May," May 31, 2005, Vatican.va.

4. Gregory of Nazianzus, Oration 45.1.

5. See *Lumen Gentium*, par. 53.

## Conclusion

1. Jean-Pierre Torrell, OP, *St. Thomas Aquinas, Volume 1: The Person and His Work*, trans. Robert Royal (The Catholic University of America Press, 1996), 279–289. Originally from *Expositio in symbol*, art. 4, nos. 920–924.

# About the Author

Sister Mary Magdalene entered the Dominican Monastery of Our Lady of the Rosary in 2009. She made Solemn Profession on January 1, 2015.